Pioneers, Farmers, and Patriots:
Roots in New England

Pioneers, Farmers, and Patriots: Roots in New England

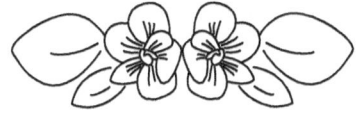

by Priscilla L. Partridge

OAK HOLLOW PRESS | WATSONVILLE, CALIFORNIA

About the author: Priscilla L. Partridge previously edited and published *The Humanitarian Gene 1891–1922, Letters and Diaries by Ernest C. Partridge, Winona G. Partridge, Mary L. Graffam and Edward G. Partridge* (2014).

Published by Oak Hollow Press, California 95076
Oakhollowpress@gmail.com

Copyright ©2025 by Priscilla L. Partridge. All rights reserved. This book or any portion thereof may not be reproduced or used in any manner whatsoever without express written permission of the author. Revised January 2026.

ISBN   978-0-9908155-3-2

Library of Congress Control Number: 2025916907

Figures are the work of the author. Photos, images, or quoted material not specified otherwise are from the collection of the author.

Type is set in Linux Libertine and Edita.
Book and cover design by Julia Warner.

CONTENTS

Preface vii
Acknowledgements ix
List of Figures xi
List of Maps xiii

Introduction 1
Chapter 1 Laura's Story 3
Chapter 2 The Ingalls 21
Chapter 3 The Brown Men Hold their Ground 39
Chapter 4 The Adventures of Ezra Jones, Laura's Grandfather ... 51
Chapter 5 The Sally Vignettes... Fowler-Davis-Banfill 71
Chapter 6 The Sally Vignettes... Youngman and Jones 93
Chapter 7 The Sally Vignettes... Safford and Everett 113
Chapter 8 Mim's Story: A Descendant of Pioneers, Farmers, and Patriots 129
Index 161

Preface

This book provides the opportunity to share the materials and information I have gathered on the ancestors of my paternal grandmother, Miriam Lucretia Ingalls. She was very dear to me and my siblings, and I cherish my memories of time spent with her as I am sure my siblings do as well.

Much has been written by and about the family she married into. Yet Miriam's roots contain interesting, adventurous, and talented individuals. Over the years, this research has resulted in two articles published in the genealogical journal, *Vermont Genealogy*. For ease of readers, I have not sourced all the facts I have accumulated, particularly since much of that information is available at online databases, historical societies, and archives. However, End Notes can be found at the end of each chapter to recognize specific or difficult to find sources, and to aid readers who would like to learn more. Materials not sourced, including photographs, screenshots, and ephemera, are from the author's personal collection. The figures are the author's work and any photos taken by the author are noted.

To fill out the life and times of most women in the early years of our country requires one to follow the vital records, land records, and published materials that discuss fathers and husbands. Though it may seem that much of this book focuses on the men in the family, it was out of necessity to use the available resources to provide context for the women. How wonderful it would be to actually hear these early pioneer women relate the stories of their lives and travels!

A recent trip through the towns mentioned in this book provided me with invaluable perspective on the places these forebears lived. Amesbury, Mass. is situated on the Merrimack River roughly 10 miles from the Atlantic Ocean. The Powow River flows into the Merrimack where the mouth holds a town park and the historic Union Congregational Church on one side and a marina on the other. Amesbury was an appropriate place for the forefathers to farm and to ply the trades associated with lumbering and shipbuilding. Taking a short drive north to Kingston, N.H., the Powow River spills over the Trickling Falls Dam which is mentioned in Davis family land deeds. Traveling west across New Hampshire as our ancestors did, and crossing over the Connecticut River into the hilly town of Bradford, I was able to see the appeal of the flat river frontage land for farming. Some ancestors remained in the hilly and woody town of Corinth, while others went north to Morristown and Hyde Park.

If these stories spark an interest in family history and inspire the reader to join the hunt to locate lost or little known ancestors, wonderful and welcome! Family research is a treasure hunt. But most importantly, may you, the reader, simply enjoy these stories about people, places, and times past.

P.L.P. August 2025

Acknowledgements

In appreciation to all the people I have contacted over the course of these investigations but are not mentioned here, I wish to thank all the employees and volunteers in libraries, historical organizations and museums, large and small, who assist folks like me in our quests to learn about people, places and events from long ago.

More specifically, the in situ research by Monica Heath of Hyde Park provided the direction I needed to continue following the Jones family lineage. A DNA match to Wayne Jones provided further impetus to find the missing link. Many thanks go to the Morristown Historical Society for allowing me to peruse through old newspapers stored at the Noyes House Museum. The Corinth Selectboard and Norm Collette, Town Historian, kindly provided me with the 1790 map showing the Davis lots in early Corinth. Michelle Emerle and the Hollis Historical Society (N.H.) have eagerly assisted with Youngman family research. Michael Dwyer, past editor of *Vermont Genealogy*, provided invaluable guidance in my early research on the Jones and Youngman families. The Gill (Mass.) Historical Commission and Peter Weis of Northfield Mount Hermon School were most helpful in fleshing out the late teenage years of the Brown siblings.

Many thanks to my dear friend, Trisha Kett, for reading the draft and sharing her editorial expertise. I am grateful to my research companions and cousin-friends, Sheryl Marcoux and Nancy Runyon, who, in addition to sharing the adventures of genealogy with me, also read a draft and expressed their enthusiasm for the project.

I would like to thank my book and cover designer, Julia Warner, for transforming my personal tribute to my grandmother into its final form.

And last but not least, I acknowledge and thank my husband, for his valued research and editorial assistance on my genealogical adventures, for his enjoyable companionship on our travels and at home, and his unwavering love.

LIST OF FIGURES

Figure 2. Parents of Laura Mary Brown and George Everett Ingalls 27

Figure 3. Line of Descent to Ira A. Brown 43

Figure 4. Line of Descent to Mary M. Jones 53

Figure 5-1. Line of Descent to Miriam Colby 74

Figure 5-2. Line of Descent to Joshua Davis 80

Figure 5-3. Line of Descent to Sally Banfill 85

Figure 6. Line of Descent to Salley Youngman 96

Figure 7. Line of Descent to George W. Everett through Three Sallys 115

LIST OF MAPS

Map 3 42
Partial image of Morrisville, Vermont, looking southwest. Geo. E. Norris, 1889 (Brockton, Mass.) G3754.M65A3. Map reproduction courtesy of the Norman B. Leventhal Map & Education Center at the Boston Public Library.

Map 4 59
Partial Plan of Lamoille Co., Vermont, 1876, J.B. Beers & Co., (H.W. Burgett & Co., New York) 4633.073; from David Rumsey Map Collection, David Rumsey Map Center, Stanford Libraries, accessed 4/2025.

Map 5-1 75
Partial Plan of Orange Co., Vermont, 1876, J.B. Beers & Co., (H.W. Burgett & Co., New York) 4633.036; from David Rumsey Map Collection, David Rumsey Map Center, Stanford Libraries, accessed 4/2025.

Map 5-2 82-83
James Whitelaw map 1790. Adapted from *History of Corinth*, Vermont 1764-1964, (Corinth, Vt.: Town of Corinth, 1995); courtesy of Town Selectboard, May 2025.

Map 6-1 95
Map of Hollis, N.H., by E.J. Colburn in *History of the Town of Hollis, New Hampshire. From its First Settlement to the Year 1879*, Samuel T. Worcester, (Boston: A. Williams & Co., 1879), facing title page.

Map 6-2 106
Lamoille County with Highgate and Hydespark circled. Vermont (cropped), 1796, J. Reid and W. Winterbotham (John Reid, New York) 0845.007; from David Rumsey Map Collection, David Rumsey Map Center, Stanford Libraries, accessed 4/2025.

Map 6-3 107
Orange County with Hydespark and Washington circled. Vermont (cropped), 1796, J. Reid and W. Winterbotham (John Reid, New York) 0845.007; from David Rumsey Map Collection, David Rumsey Map Center, Stanford Libraries, accessed 4/2025.

Map 7 118
Partial view of City and Vicinity of Boston Massachusetts (Brighton), 1852, F.G. Sidney and R.P. Smith (J.B. Shields, Boston) 5464.002; from David Rumsey Map Collection, David Rumsey Map Center, Stanford Libraries, accessed 4/2025.

Introduction

Miriam Ingalls' ancestral roots reach far into northern Vermont, and before that New Hampshire and Massachusetts, from whence the forebears of Brown, Jones, Davis, and Youngman came. Her mother, Laura Mary Brown, left Vermont and Massachusetts, to settle in New Hampshire as a new wife to George Everett Ingalls. The young Ingalls couple left New England for Kansas and then Ohio where Miriam was born. This collection of stories begins with anecdotes about Laura Mary Brown who left New England with her husband and their first child to follow his career in the midwestern states. The stories close with Laura's daughter, Miriam, known as "Mim" for much of her life, who returned with her own family to the land of her roots.

In between, we view generations of families who fervently supported the formation of our democracy, the protection of this new government and its people, and the cause of abolition. Many families continued to move into less populated areas which required arduous physical exertion to make the new homesteads comfortable for families. The more recent generations can be studied through primary materials like photographs, letters and various ephemera. As we move back in time personal materials become less common. The community news columns of local papers do lend some flavor and excitement for the mid-to late nineteenth century predecessors. Prior to that, however, we must follow the existing vital, land, and probate records of the men that Laura's female ancestors associated with-fathers, husbands, brothers, sons-to learn about the lives of these women. Who were their family members? Where did the women and their families live? What were the men's occupations? What causes did they champion? The following narratives aim to provide insight into the life experiences of people from whom we descend.

Chapter 1
Laura's Story

Laura Mary Brown's Wedding

Laura Mary Brown was the middle "Laura," most likely named after her aunt Laura E. Brown. Her brother Clayton H. Brown honored both his sister and his aunt by naming his second daughter, Laura.

Laura's parents, Ira A. Brown and Mary Jones Brown Darling, were deceased by the time of her marriage but her Aunt Laura Brown Moody hosted the wedding of Laura Mary Brown to George Everett Ingalls. (See Figure 2.) The guest list for Laura's June 27, 1899 wedding included over 200 people - a phenomenal number considering Hyde Park was in the Northern Kingdom of Vermont and not a metropolitan community. However, the ceremony was held in Salem, Massachusetts so it is questionable as to how many Vermont folks actually attended.

Family members that were invited included her grandfather Ezra Jones and her mother's sisters and their families, her uncle Wilbur Jones and his family, and her Brown

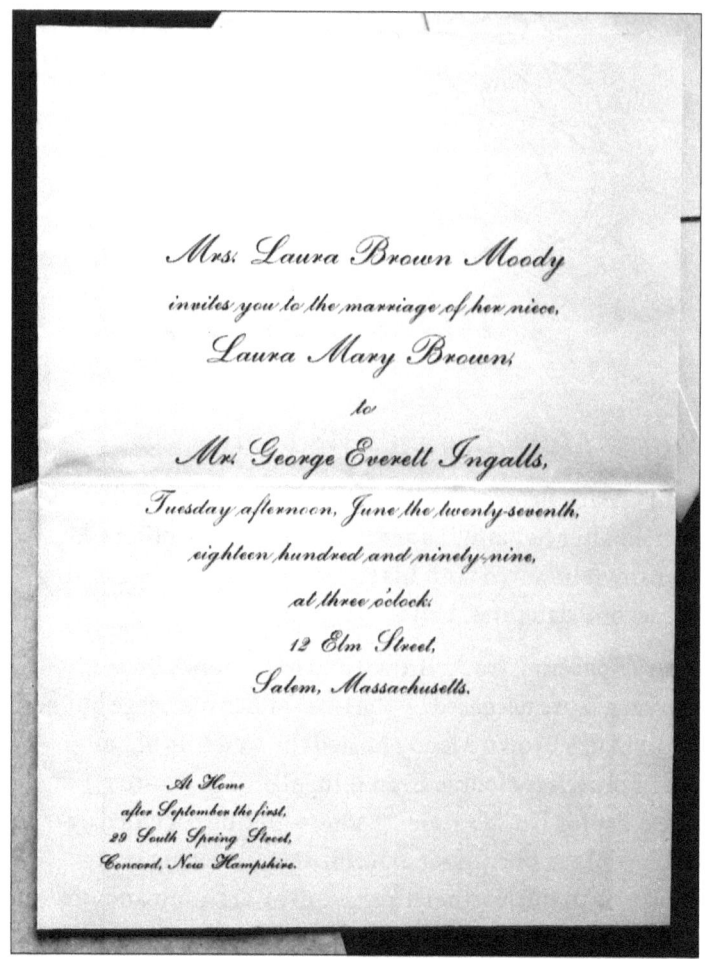

Wedding invitation for Laura Mary Brown, 27 June 1899, Salem, Mass.

14. Mr. & Mrs. Sidney Bartlett & Family.
    Garfield, Vt.
15. Mr. E. C. Jones. Garfield, Vt.
16. Mrs Elsie A. Taylor. 33 Sargeants Ave,
                                Somerville, Mass.
17. Mr. & Mrs. George Kingsbury
18. Mr. Joseph Tisdale
    Miss Bertha Tisdale,
                    328 Cypress St, Manchester

153. Miss Eleanor Waters
154. Mr. & Mrs. Roy R. Hatch
155. Rev. & Mrs. Roscoe Nelson

26. Mr. J. C. Sanborn
    Mr. Varnum Sanborn
27. Miss Sadie Sanborn

Partial guest list for the wedding of Laura Mary Brown, 27 June 1899.

aunts (half-sisters of her father Ira). Friends, like Mr. J.C. Sanborn, Aunt Laura's neighbor who had provided housing and employment to her brother, were invited. In spite of a difficult childhood, Laura included her stepfather, A.P. Darling, her stepbrothers and stepsisters, and her two half-sisters. And of course, on the list were Mr. & Mrs. C. H. Brown, Laura's surviving brother Clayton and wife. Clayton entered Mt. Hermon School in 1893 as a student and was later employed by the school. His wife Beulah Wright was a student of Northfield Seminary and they married in 1896. Additional guests invited were Mr. and Mrs. Roy Hatch – Laura's friend Grace Josephine Pitts and her new husband – who had married in 1897 and resided in Gill, Mass.

Sometime after turning fifteen, Laura went to live with her Aunt Laura Moody in Methuen, Mass. Aunt Laura saw that her namesake received the necessary schooling to be a teacher. Laura attended the Salem Normal School where high school graduates were trained in Pedagogy and curriculum. Salem Normal School was founded in 1854 at the corner of Broad and Summer Streets and was the fourth such school started by the General Court of Massachusetts because Salem was one of the cities determined to be in need of teachers. Salem Normal School later morphed into Salem Teachers College, then Salem State College, and is now called Salem State University.

After graduating from Salem Normal School in 1896, Laura left Methuen, Mass. to begin her career as teacher in a one-room schoolhouse in Gill, Mass., known as North School, near the Mount Hermon School campus. The schoolhouse still stands but is currently serving as a private residence. It is likely Laura went to Gill because her brother, Clayton,

REGISTER OF STUDENTS.
1896-97.

GRADUATES, — JUNE, 1896.
Of the Advanced Course.

Alice Minerva Abbott,	Newmarket, N. H.
Julia Clarke Carleton,	Danvers.

Of the Two Years' Course.

Ardelle Abbott,	Somerville.
Charlotte May Baine,	Swampscott.
Mary Gertrude Brogan,	Lawrence.
Laura May Brown,	Morrisville, Vt.

State Normal School at Salem, "Forty-Third Year of the State Normal School at Salem, Mass., 1896-1897."[1]

was working as farm manager at Mount Hermon School. But most certainly Laura met her betrothed, George E. Ingalls, while she was living in Methuen, Mass.

A Dedicated Son - Clayton H. Brown

Clayton H. Brown was ten months old and Ira Raymond Brown was barely two when their father Ira A. Brown died. Their mother, Mary, was pregnant with their sister Laura, and may not have even known she was carrying another child when her husband died. By July of 1876 when Laura was born, the 22-year-old widow had the sole care of three children under age three. It is not surprising that in less than two years Mary married again to a widower with four mother-less children, three of them less than ten years younger than herself. Alonzo Putnam Darling was a first cousin to Mary's mother, Chloe Haskins, and together Mary and A.P. had a son and two daughters of their own.

Mary Jones Brown Darling had faced numerous challenges in the years prior to her death. In 1890, the Alonzo Darling home in Morristown burned and the family moved out to Elmore where they rented a home from Alonzo's sister, Mrs. Woodbury. In February 1892, Mary and Alonzo went to Hyde Park to visit her ill father. No mention is made of her mother or in what month in 1892 her mother died. The next month, Mary and Alonzo's son, Ernest, became sick with malignant diptheria and died a week later just shy of his twelfth birthday. Then, their daughter Blanch became ill with "diptheretic sore throat" causing son Ernest's funeral to be postponed.

Young Clayton's life in the household of his stepfather was somber if not outright unbearable. On the day of his mother's death, 14 May 1892, Clayton went to work at Gray's mill in Pleasant Valley. Mr. Darling and family attended his oldest daughter's tenth wedding anniversary celebration while Mary Darling stayed at home. Clayton returned home to find his mother ill. A doctor was not available and she died that evening.

Since Laura was "stopping for a season [in Elmore] with the afflicted family of her mother," it seems Laura had already moved to Mass. and was on school vacation when her mother fell ill and died. The burial and funeral took place on May 18 and was described in detail in the Elmore column of the News and Citizen on May 26. Laura and several Brown family members were mentioned, but son Clayton and Mary's parents, Ezra and Chloe Jones, were not.

The following day, Friday, May 27, Clayton moved to Methuen, Mass. to join Laura in the home of their father's sister, Laura E. Brown Moody, who had no children of her own. Laura and Clayton were orphans and alone - their older brother, Ira, had died about five years earlier, at the age of fifteen. Aunt Laura oversaw and paid for Laura's education and was determined to rescue Clayton from the farm and his unfortunate stepfather. She successfully set him up with a family in Methuen where he drove a horse team and worked as a janitor for the Baptist Society. Aunt Laura began to plan Clayton's education by investigating schools and sending for catalogs.

After receiving the catalog from Mount Hermon located in Gill, Mass., Aunt Laura wrote to the principal in the spring of 1893 describing Clayton:

> *His father died when he was a very small child leaving the mother with three little ones and Clayton, from an*

Looking at the town of Elmore, Vt. from Elmore State Park beach. Photo by author.

Elmore Mountain with hiking trail to Fire Tower. Photo by author.

early age has been very mindful of her and refused to go away where he could go to school because he knew she would suffer in many ways without him, one year ago she died and he came to me and has been working, saving his money...

Aunt Laura goes on to say that she cannot help financially this year as she is educating his sister at present and that her research shows that Mount Hermon is the only school that he can afford. Mr. J.C. Sanborn of Methuen, Mass., in whose home Clayton had been most recently living, sent a supporting letter to Mr. Cutler at Mount Hermon in June 1893. "I have always found him faithful, trustworthy, industrious and absolutely free from bad habits. He is quiet, gentlemanly and intelligent. He needs the training your school can give. I believe he will prove himself worthy..." Nathan Bailey, the pastor of the First Baptist Church, Methuen, Mass. also wrote of his "excellent character" and spirituality–"a thorough Christian."

As part of his application to Mount Hermon School, Clayton wrote a letter to Mr. Cutler telling how he had had little schooling as a child. "I have always lived a long distance from school and my Stept father [sic] thought that I did not need an education and so when I attempted to go I could only remain a few days when he would take me out to do some work. I did not like to leave my mother and so staid with her until she died."

Upon Clayton's acceptance, Aunt Laura corresponded with Mr. Cutler regarding expenses, supplies, incidentals, tuition payments and his progress. Clayton appears to have attended class regularly his first year but he began to have difficulty his second year. On January 22, 1895, Aunt Laura wrote to Mr. Cutler:

> *Dear Sir, I wish to write you in regard to Clayton. He has been discontented and has had very little ambition about study since going back to school in September and knowing this I was not much surprised when I saw the paper you sent me. I received a letter from him saying that he is working on the farm. This I do not understand.*

She wished Mr. Cutler to have a talk with Clayton and so expanded on Clayton's family life history.

> *After the death of his Father his mother married a shiftless man whose name is Darling and who is a brother of Mrs. Woodbury the wife of Governor Woodbury of Vermont. They had been renting a farm owned by Mr. Woodbury when Clayton's mother died leaving two little girls. At this time Mr. Darling's son undertook to run the farm with his sister as housekeeper and caring for the little ones.*

Apparently, Clayton's older step-siblings were caring for the younger Darling half-sisters. Aunt Laura continued: "About three weeks ago Clayton received a letter from one of Mr. Darling's neighbors saying that the son had gotten into trouble and had left for Canada and they thought Clayton ought to come and do the work. This is a scheme gotten up by Mr. Darling. He would not write to Clayton himself on my account. He will not work and he abused Clayton all through his childhood." Aunt Laura then assured Mr. Cutler that she is confident that the little girls will be taken care of by Mrs. Woodbury. Clayton was not necessary for their care.[2]

Laura's childhood was probably not idyllic either, however she invited her stepfather and step brothers and her half-sisters to her wedding. The two siblings likely formed a close bond due to their ages and adverse life events and contentious household conditions. Since Clayton arrived at Gill in September 1893 to attend Mt. Hermon School, and Laura took an opportunity to teach in Gill upon her graduation in 1895, it follows that Laura wished to be near her brother.

Northfield Neighbors – Roy and Grace Hatch

Evidently at some point in her life, Laura Ingalls acquired the nickname "Brownie." From her home in Ohio, Laura maintained a relationship across the distance to Massachusetts with Roy and Grace Hatch. At age 19, Roy Hatch was hired as the groundskeeper for Mount Hermon School in Gill, Mass. Roy was the same age as Clayton who began working on the school farm in 1894 while he was a student. In 1897, Roy married Grace Josephine Pitts, Laura's friend from Massachusetts who was ten years older than he.

According to George L. Partridge's autobiography, *Auto by Pat*, Grace was a friend of Laura's who came to visit her in Gill. Grace was introduced to Roy Hatch and "a romance developed." George reminisced that "Roy was a remarkable young man who started as a teamster, worked up to be a physics teacher, and eventually an outstanding physics

Laura Brown Ingalls, December 25, 1920.

Laura M. Brown Ingalls circa 1926.

teacher and head of the Science Department."[3] Roy began adulthood as a farm worker as did Laura's brother Clayton and improved his lot in life to become a respected teacher. Clayton also moved upward from the Mount Hermon farm to manage a large farm for a wealthy New York family. Clayton then became a conductor on the Connecticut Railway and a part-time policeman. The two men surely had qualities and character in common making the marriage of Grace to Roy an enjoyable benefit for Laura.

The Hatches retired to 122 Birnam Road in Northfield, Mass. Nearly fifty years after Laura and Grace became friends, the Hatches learned that "Brownie's" daughter was coming to Northfield and was to live in the house next door. Grace insisted that Roy clean up the front yard of 124 Birnam Road as a welcoming gift. Miriam's husband, George Partridge, had accepted a teaching position at the Northfield Girls School and had leased the home on Birnam Road as of June 1944. A shortage of teachers enabled the already "retired" Roy to be the physics teacher for Miriam's son during his high school years at Mount Hermon School. During a visit to her son and daughter-in-law, Winona Partridge noted in her diary on May 16, 1946: "Miriam and I attended a tea at Mrs. Hatch's in my honor."

Miriam's recipe box holds a recipe for rolls from her mother's dear friend, Grace Pitts Hatch.

A recipe for rolls from Miriam's recipe box, from Grace Pitts Hatch.

Northfield Neighbors – The Comptons

Moving to Birnam Road also held a Partridge familial connection for George and Miriam – a nearby home was occupied by Carl and Ruth Compton. Mr. & Mrs. Compton were a newly married couple in 1918 when they travelled with Ernest Partridge on the Russia expedition to provide relief and aid to Armenian genocide survivors. When the Russian Revolution broke out in Siberia, Ernest returned to the U.S. via China and Japan, whereas Carl and Ruth Compton stayed on with the YMCA to work with Russian and Czech soldiers in Siberia.

Later, Mr. Compton became President of Anatolia College of Turkey, which had been relocated to Greece in 1925. The Comptons were on furlough when WWII broke out so they moved to Northfield where Carl taught at Mount Hermon School. They returned to Greece shortly after Miriam and

George arrived on Birnam Road, but returned to Northfield for retirement and lived there until 1979. Miriam and George built their retirement home on North Lane in 1971 which made the Comptons and Partridges "across the street" neighbors for eight years!

Endnotes

1. State Normal School at Salem, "Forty-Third Year of the State Normal School at Salem, Mass., 1896-1897," (1897), College Catalogs., 78, http://digitalcommons.salemstate.edu/college_catalogs/78. Note: Laura "May" Brown is an error.

2. Above quotes and much of the general information on Clayton Brown came from #1450MH, x1893-1894, Archives of Northfield Mount Hermon, Gill, Mass., Sept 2017.

3. George L. Partridge, *Auto By Pat*, (Amityville, N.Y.: Vining Press, 1985).

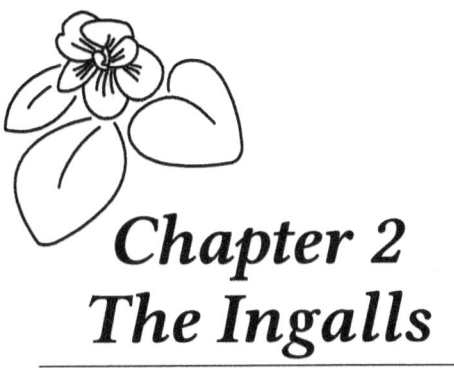

Chapter 2
The Ingalls

Laura and George Everett...
Their Life Together

Laura fled Vermont and the difficult life with her stepfather prior to her mother's death. She received her teacher's training in coastal Salem, Mass. but went west across Massachusetts for a teaching position. During her married life, she resided in New Hampshire, Kansas, and Ohio. Laura may well have had the wandering bug like her great-grandfather John Jones–he was born in New Hampshire to an early settler family of Amesbury, Massachusetts. The Browns had been Vermonters for several generations and New Hampshire folk before that. Similarly, husband George Everett Ingalls' immigrant ancestor, Henry Ingalls arrived in Massachusetts circa 1650 and was one of the first settlers of Andover, Mass. Ingalls ancestors then moved to Chester, New Hampshire for several generations.

George Everett Ingalls was the middle child of John Addison Gurley (variously known as John J., John G., Gurley J.) Ingalls and Lucretia Underhill Everett, and was born in Methuen, Mass. George was named after his maternal grandfather George W. Everett who was born in Watertown, Mass. and died in Methuen, Mass when his namesake grandchild was two years old. George W. Everett lived in Chester, New Hampshire for some years during which time he was a member of the N.H. House of Representatives. Lucretia Underhill Everett was born in Chester.

At the young age of 19, George Everett Ingalls bought lot 352 in Walnut Grove Cemetery likely initiated by the death of his brother Percy Howe Ingalls who had died that year (1891) from typhoid. Eventually George's parents, his first-born daughter Marion, and wife Laura were laid to rest in Walnut Grove along with other Ingalls relatives.

Young George was living in Bellows Falls, Vermont in 1894 when he received the following poem for his 22nd birthday:

> *From his home in Massachusetts*
> *From the grand historic Bay-State*
> *From the county long-called Essex*
> *Essex County, famed for witches*
>   *In the days of long ago*
>
> *Went a youth of two and twenty,*
> *Went he forth in earliest Spring time,*
> *Went he forth in search for silver,*
> *Silver coin wherewith to purchase*
> *Shoes, and shirts, and bread with butter;*
>   *'mongst the Vermont hills of snow.*
>
> *Long he tarried by the river*
> *Long thro' April, May 'til June.*
> *June, the month of blooming roses-*
> *Told his friends in Essex County*
> *Loving friends who missed him daily*
>   *That a birthday gift was due.*

Lucretia Everett Ingalls and John Addison Gurley Ingalls, c1864. Possibly their wedding photo.

Then in earnest loving conclave
Pondered parents, sister too,
Pondered saying, "Shall we send him
Birthday cake – a loving token
Token of unchanged affection
    Token of remembrance true."
"Send it not" they quickly murmured.
"Send no gross materials food
To the land of maple sugar,
To the town among the mountains
    To the Vermont wanderer!"

So they gathered daintier mind-food
Gathered Drummonds greatest things
Gathered "Reveries" by firelight
Neckties, kerchiefs having eyes.
Blushing strawberry, actual first fruit
For the youth of two and twenty
    In the town of Bellows Falls.

Called him from his daily paper
Called to add a bright half dollar
To the birthday gift in June.

Forth they go – the loving tokens
Forth to cheer the absent one.
Forth to carry sweet reminders
Of the home in Essex County
'Twixt the Merrimac and Spicket
In the old historic Bay State
Where they hung the Salem witches
    In the days of long ago.

–Lucretia Longfellow

The Ingalls

Did Lucretia Underhill Ingalls know that in colonial New England two of her ancestors, Mehitable Braybrook Downing and Susanna North Martin, were accused of witchcraft? And that Susannah Martin was hung in 1692? Did she know that her husband, John A. G. Ingalls, descended from another accused witch, Rebeckah (--) Chamberlain, who died in prison?

George Everett Ingalls made a gift of a Bible to Laura in which he inscribed the following: "Laura M. Brown From Everett October 26, 1898." The current generation does not know if he went by Everett at work or if this was only a family moniker. At the time of George's betrothment and wedding, he was employed in the position of Secretary by the B & M Railroad YMCA (Young Men's Christian Association) in Concord, New Hampshire. He attended a convention in Fort Wayne, Indiana in 1898 and brought back a ribbon. Laura tucked that ribbon into her Bible where it can be found to this day.

About twenty-five years earlier, members of the Cleveland, Ohio, YMCA along with railroad executives were concerned for the welfare of railroad employees whose choices for food and lodging when traveling most often consisted of saloons and brothels. The Railroad YMCA created convenient and safe rooms near the terminals where railroad employees could relax, eat, enjoy entertainment and games, consider religious principles, all without the influence of alcohol. The "secretary" role was similar to a missionary. The B & M Railroad Department YMCA where George was employed was organized in 1895 and situated in a building across the street from the Concord railroad station on Storrs Street. This wooden building was replaced in 1907 with a multistory brick structure. George and

Laura Brown Ingalls' Bible.

The Ingalls

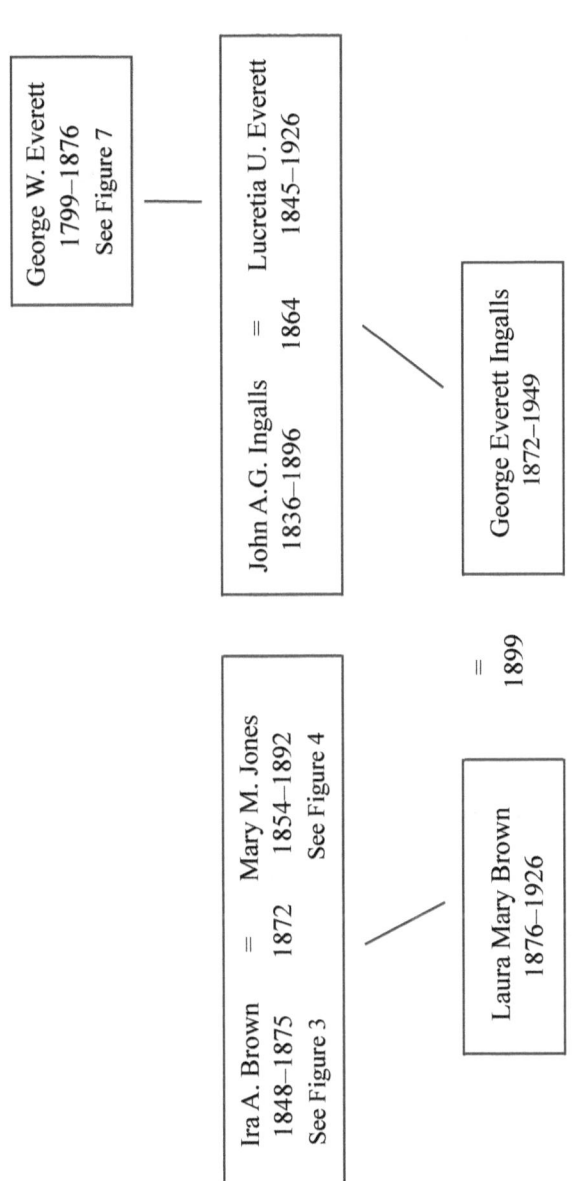

Figure 2. Parents of Laura Mary Brown and George Everett Ingalls.

Laura's home on 29 South Spring Street was about a half mile away.

George and Laura Ingalls moved to the Kansas City suburb of Argentine, Kansas by 1901 where they suffered the loss of a baby daughter, Marion Brown Ingalls. The next year Harold "Pete" Brown Ingalls was born. George was secretary to the Argentine Atchison Topeka and Santa Fe (ATSF) Railroad YMCA which had only been operating since 1899.

By 1905, George's YMCA employment brought him to Cleveland, Ohio where Railroad YMCA had started in 1872. The 1920 census shows that he had achieved Executive Secretary level. George's second son, Robert, desired to take over the Secretary position from his father at his retirement. According to Robert Ingalls' son, Carl, the position was given over to someone else precipitating Robert's move to Arizona with his family. George's eldest son, Harold, was also employed by the YMCA for a time during his life.

Following the move to Ohio, Miriam Lucretia, Robert Harding, and Christine R. joined the family. Miriam was born in 1905 in Bellevue, Ohio, before the family relocated to the east side of Cleveland. Federal censuses and city directories show that the George Ingalls family lived in at least six homes, all rented, by the time Laura succumbed to tuberculosis in 1926.

Laura's photo album provides a look inside her family life. The family spent a summer tent camping and canoeing on Lake Erie. In 1910 they went to the YMCA camp on Silver Bay in Lake George, New York. One summer they visited a camp named Aurora. The album shows photos taken in Missouri and New Mexico, and closer to home – Wade Park in Cleveland. The assortment of photographs includes the

B & M Railroad Department Y.M.C.A. 1895. With permission of the New Hampshire Historical Society.

Christine, Robert, Miriam, Harold circa 1913.

Young Miriam at 940 E. 150th NE, Cleveland, OH with Christine, probable cousin, and Harold, circa 1913.

Ingalls children and the group images likely include extended family—possibly brother Clayton and Alice Brown and 3 children; sister Mattie Morse Aldrich-Ames and her family; or even Laura's half-sister's and their families. Matriarch Mrs. John A.G. Ingalls (Lucretia Everett), who died in January of 1926 while visiting in Ohio, may well have been one of the subjects.

A sampling of Laura's handwriting appears in Miriam's high school autograph book:

> *Before God's footstool to confess*
> *A poor soul knelt, and bowed his head;*
> *"I failed" he cried. The master said:*
> *"Thou didst thy best – that is success!"*
> *Your affectionate Mother*
>
> Laura B. Ingalls
>
> Mar. 30, 1921

Several years after Laura's death, George Everett Ingalls purchased a farm on Hobart Road on the border between Willoughby and Kirtland, Ohio. That year, 1929, the farm was the venue for three family weddings—daughter Christine married Ralph M. McKay on May 9; father George E. married Miss Lelia Snyder on May 20; and daughter Miriam married George L. Partridge on July 27.

Numerous family gatherings were held at the Kirtland Farm. George Everett signed their annual Christmas card, usually a depiction of the farm, as "Mom and Dad." In her enjoyable family history, Lelia wrote of her husband by his middle name "Everett" rather than George.[1] Apparently, he preferred his loved ones to use his middle name. This middle name tradition continued with a grandson and a great grand-daughter.

> Before God's footstool to confess
> A poor soul knelt, and bowed his head;
> "I failed," he cried: "The Master said:
> "Thou didst thy best—that is success!"
>
> Your affectionate mother,
> Laura B. Ingalls.
> Mar. 30, 1921.

From Miriam's high school autograph book 1920–1922.

Robert, Miriam, Christine, Harold.

clockwise l. to r. Miriam, Christine, Harold, Robert.

As Harold Ingalls, who went by "Pete" within the family, began his own family he wrote a personal and thankful letter to his father, which included his mother (Mother) and stepmother (Mom).

Thanksgiving, 1939

Thank you, Dad –

Thanks for what you are and always have been. Thanks for the fine start you gave me, for the kind home which you and Mother created, for the ways you kept the highest ideals ever before us kids, for the ample provision you made for our needs when it was terribly hard to do so Thanks for you sense of humor, for the way you entered into our joys and made yourself a part of our activities; perhaps we resented it at times or thought you a bit ridiculous to be playing kid with us of the mature age of sixteen or seventeen – but now we are older we know better and appreciate it all. Thanks for you example of hard work, and for the willingness to take on extra work after your regular work was done – work that kept the home going when Mother wasn't up to it. Thanks for teaching us to do our shares, too; thanks much for that. Thanks for your courage; how on earth you managed to go ahead under the most depressing of conditions, when the load got bigger and the responsibilities more staggering, while the hope of realizing what you so dearly cherished grew dimmer and dimmer, is something that has caused me to marvel often....Thanks for encouraging us to go ahead and make our way in the world, for creating the urge to get more education, for helping us to seek jobs and do them. Thanks for making it possible for us to have so many fine experiences in our home and with the friends you brought there. Thanks for giving us a solid, sane, lasting religious background – not the least part of which

The Ingalls

Miriam Lucretia Ingalls and George Lewis Partridge married on 27 July 1929, Collinwood, Ohio.

Miriam with her father George E. Ingalls and sister Christine I. McKay.

is your own faith. Thanks for holding us loosely until we were strong enough to stand alone, and thanks for letting go when we were – while you stood by always ready to help in any way you could in the latter years...Thanks for your kindness and breadth of outlook that drew from a deep sympathy. Thanks for your fairness and your sincerity...Thanks for everything and more.

And Mom, thanks to you –

I don't suppose you have any idea what a difficult job you undertook. If there ever were four kids who loved their mother more, the fact has been well concealed. You were wise enough to know what we knew – that no one could ever take Mother's place – and you set about to make a place for yourself. Make it? Well, perhaps win it is better said...I shall not try to summarize or itemize – just take a blank check and make it out to yourself in terms of unlimited thanks for what you have done for all of us and for Dad and for what you have been and are to all five of us (and the in-laws, too)... Many, many thanks for everything.

George Everett Ingalls and Lelia Snyder Ingalls were laid to rest nearby their Ohio farm in South Kirtland Cemetery.

The Ingalls family line can be tracked back to the immigrant ancestor Edmund Ingalls who came from Skirbeck, Lincolnshire, England to Salem, Mass. with Governor Endicott's Colony in 1628. Ingalls drowned in 1648 when he and the horse he was traveling on fell through a bridge into the Saugus River. Much can be learned about the early Ingalls families in published works. [2]

The Ingalls

Patriot ancestors of George Everett Ingalls include Israel Everett, Thomas Safford whose daughter Sally will be discussed in a later chapter, John Underhill, Stephen Lufkin, Humphrey Choate, on his maternal line and David Sanborn, Jr. and Jonathan Powers on the Ingalls line.

Endnotes

1. Lelia Snyder Ingalls, *Those who have gone before, to the Grandsons and Granddaughters of Edmund and Annette*, (unpublished, c1930), Partridge Family Collection.

2. Charles D. Burleigh, *The Genealogy and History of the Ingalls Family in America: giving the descendants of Edmund Ingalls who settled at Lynn, Mass. in 1629*, (Malden, Mass.: G.E. Dunbar, 1903). Also, William Richard Cutter, *Genealogical & Personal Memoirs Relating to the families of Boston & Eastern Massachusetts*, Vol IV (New York: Lewis Historical Publishing Company, 1908). Both are available online at archive.org.

Chapter 3
The Brown Men Hold Their Ground

The Family of Ira A. Brown, Laura's Father

Ira A. Brown died before Laura was born leaving a pregnant wife and two sons under age three. The young Brown family had been living in Hyde Park, Lamoille County, Vermont, where the sons were born. Ira's death was not recorded, causing one to consider that his death may have been from some kind of farming, lumbering, or sawmill accident. Probate Court awarded the widow Mary Brown the ownership of 36 acres in Hyde Park that Ira A. Brown had bought from his father-in-law, Ezra C. Jones, sometime after 1868. Mary Brown then sold lot No. 44, the College lot, in December of 1876, whereupon the new owners agreed to assume the balance of the mortgage and to continue paying the annual rent to the University at Burlington.

Ira was born in Wolcott, Vt., a small town named for Oliver Wolcott, a signer of the Declaration of Independence, and located in a valley formed by the Lamoille River. Wolcott is about ten miles northeast of Hyde Park and the village of Morrisville where Mary Jones spent much of her childhood. At the census of June 1870, Ira and Mary resided in the same home in the Cadys Falls neighborhood of Hyde Park. The head of house, Alger Baldwin, and Ira Brown, age 22, both worked in a saw mill. Mary, age 17, was listed as a domestic servant. Ira Brown and Mary Jones married 7 March 1872 in Hyde Park. When their first son, also named Ira, was born in 1873, the father's occupation was "farmer." Clayton arrived in December 1874. Laura was born in Wolcott in July of 1876 and her birth record also listed Ira's occupation as farmer. Ira's headstone in Fairmount Cemetery, Wolcott, Vt. reveals that he died shortly after Laura's conception.

Harvey M. Brown and Phylinda Davis were Ira's parents. Philinda was born in Corinth, Vt., in 1810 to Nathan Davis and Sally Banfill. The families of Philinda's parents came from southeastern New Hampshire and Essex County, Massachusetts to Corinth where Harvey and Philinda were both born and later married. Philinda, however, was the second of Harvey's four wives. Harvey Brown and his family had moved north to Wolcott by 1857 when Philinda died from consumption. Ira was 9 years old. Harvey participated in real estate transactions and manufacturing before he relocated to the larger community of Morrisville (within the town of Morristown) for the final 15 years of his long life. Harvey M. Brown was a witness to the sale of Mary Jones Brown's land.

Wolcott, Vt. Railroad Depot. Currently used as the town library. Photos by author.

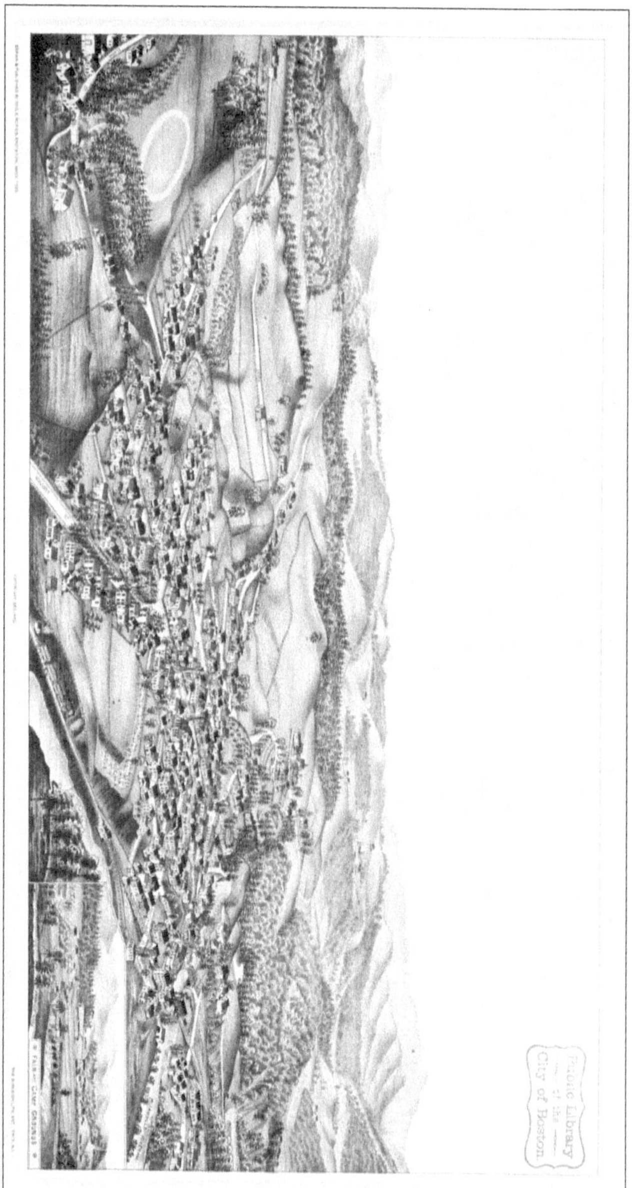

PIONEERS, FARMERS, AND PATRIOTS

Map 3. Partial image of Morrisville, Vermont, looking southwest. Courtesy of Boston Public Library.

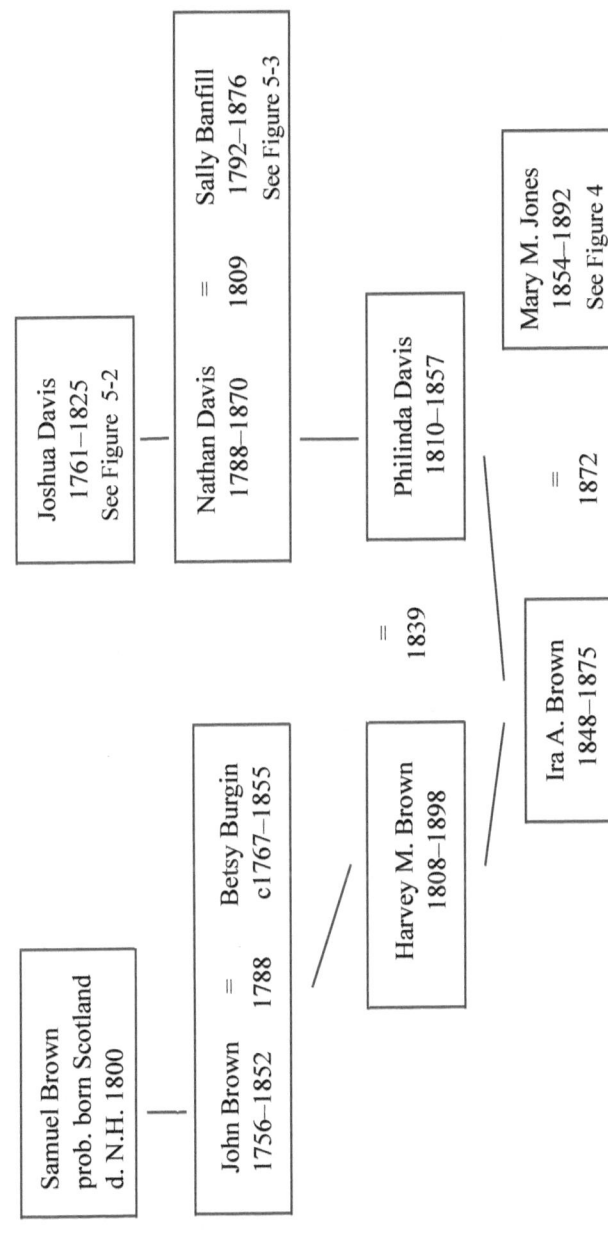

Figure 3. Line of Descent to Ira A. Brown.

Harvey's parents, John and Betsy Brown, had a large family – at least fifteen children. Harvey was one of the youngest. John Brown was born in Chester, N.H., and married Betsey Burgin in Pembroke, N.H., before settling in Corinth, Vt. In later life, they resided with various of their children in New Hampshire, Maine, and Massachusetts.

> The funeral of Harvey Brown was held last Thursday afternoon at the home of Mrs. Sleeper, his daughter. Rev. Daniel Gregory, of the Advent society, officiated and the remains were taken to Wolcott for burial. Mr. Brown was one of the oldest men in town, being nearly 90 years old.

Argus and Patriot, Wednesday, September 7 1898.

Independence/Patriotism/War of the Rebellion

Through three generations, the men in the Brown family demonstrated willingness to take up arms to assure economic and personal liberties for Americans. Samuel Brown and his son John Brown supported the American War for Independence for the Province of New Hampshire. Samuel and John were the great-great-grandfather and great-grandfather of Laura Mary Brown and her brother Clayton.

Samuel was likely an immigrant from Scotland who reportedly emigrated with two brothers, Joseph and William. Samuel and his brothers settled in Chester Woods, Rockingham Co., N.H. – an area that later was incorporated as Hooksett in Merrimack Co. Samuel owned 5th division lot 28 – land which later housed the Hooksett poor farm.[1] In

1736/7, Samuel Brown and other inhabitants of Chester, N.H. signed a petition to Governor Jonathan Belcher. The petitioners described themselves:

> *That your Petitioners, though at present Inhabitants of Chester aforsd, formerly belonged, most of them, to the Kingdom of Scotland & Ireland, where they were educated in the principles of Kirk of Scotland, for which they have great Veneration...*[2]

Samuel Brown was voted to be a member of the "Committee of Inspection or Safety" and signed the Association Test for Chester, N.H. in 1777 along with his likely brother William. The above information on Samuel was gleaned from the "History of Old Chester" by Benjamin Chase. New Hampshire war records show a Samuel Brown with military service as a private and later as a Lieutenant.

However, son John Brown volunteered in September of 1775 for two months as a private with Capt. Daniel Moore's Company to go to Winter Hill near Boston. After his commitment he returned home to Chester, N.H. Soon after, he enlisted in Capt. Andrew Suntin's Company for four months (Dec. 1775 through March 1776). Both of these companies were under the command of Col. John Stark of the 1st New Hampshire Regiment of the Continental Army.

Although John Brown enlisted again in July of 1777, he did not participate in the Battle of Bennington with Col. Stark because he had signed up with Capt. Simon Marston under the command of Col. Joseph Senter to defend Rhode Island. As a member of Capt. Marston's Company, John received salary and travel expenses for the expedition. The Americans made two unsuccessful attempts in 1777 to recapture the town and harbor of Newport from British occupation and control. After serving his commitment, John Brown was dismissed by Capt. Marston.

Congress passed The Pension Act of 1832 which allowed pensions for soldiers based on their service. At the age of 74, while living in Topsham, Vt., John Brown applied for a pension. John Brown began receiving an annual pension of $34.05 in 1836, which his widow Betsey continued to receive after his death.[3] John Brown is a verified Patriot of the Daughters of the American Revolution (DAR).

John and Betsey Brown sired eight sons, several of whom served in American conflicts. Three sons, Manly H., Samuel B., and Thomas G., served in the War of 1812. Laura's grandfather Harvey M. Brown was a small boy during that war.

Second oldest son Manly H. Brown lived in Chester, N.H. in 1840 in a household of 25 people, two of whom were engaged in agriculture. Neither the informant for the household nor the census taker wrote Manly's name in the column on page 2 for military service. However, Manly H. Brown registered as a private in the U.S. Infantry under Capt. Silas Dickinson and Col. Daniel Dana. He was 5' 9" with blue eyes, brown hair, light complexion, aged 19, and a farmer from Chester, N.H. when he enlisted on 25 June 1813. He completed his term of one year.[4]

Brother Samuel B. Brown had been a colonel of a regiment in the Vermont militia and was asked by the Governor of Vermont to escort General Marquis de Lafayette, the last surviving general of the Revolution, for part of his tour in June of 1825.[5] Samuel was 28 years old at the time. Between 1834 and 1839, Samuel left Vermont for Bangor, Maine where he lived until age 93.

> I do not now think of any other proof I can give you as only two members of the Regt to my knowlege are living.
>
> I make the above declaration of facts on the veracity of a Christian Minister, and shall make oath to the same.
>
> I have the honor to be very Respectfully your Obedient Servant,
>
> Thomas G. Brown
>
> (Com of Pensions)
> Personally appeared Thomas G. Brown

Thomas G. Brown, U.S. War 1812, Pension SO33271.[6]

Next younger brother, Thomas G. Brown, enlisted in the 31st Regiment of Vermont Volunteers during the War of 1812. Many years later, Thomas encountered difficulty obtaining a pension based on his War of 1812 service and wrote a letter to the Commissioner of Pensions in Washington dated 27 September 1878 to explain his service activities. Thomas quoted information from correspondence from his brother who served in the 31st Regiment and was receiving a pension. A that time, only his brother Manly and one other man were still living from that regiment.[7]

During the Civil War, Rev. Thomas Brown, age 61, joined the 21st Connecticut Volunteers and was known as "The Fighting Chaplain."[8] The Chaplain wrote a "required" report to the Brigadier General on the conditions of the 21st Regiment which presented their situation, not much different from other units, in an overall positive tone, considering the men were injured, sick, or stationed at fighting posts.[9]

Thomas' son, Henry B. Brown, was appointed acting assistant paymaster for the US Navy during the Civil War and was assigned to the Atlantic and Gulf region.[10]

Laura's Brown ancestors were early settlers of Hooksett, N.H, Corinth, Vt. and Bangor, Maine. The male members of the Brown family were well represented in the formation of the United States and in subsequent conflicts in American history.

End Notes

1. Duane Hamilton Hurd, ed., *History of Merrimack and Belknap counties, New Hampshire*, (Philadelphia: J.W. Lewis & Co., 1885), p364.

2. Benjamin Chase, *History of Old Chester from 1719 to 1869*, (Auburn, N.H.: author, 1869), p83.

3. Further details of John Brown's military history can be found in: 1) S*W14360, Brown, John, Revolutionary War, M804, Record Group 15 accessed at Fold3.com; 2) *The Provincial and State Papers of New Hampshire*, volumes 14-25, published by the New Hampshire State Legislature from 1867-1943 (40 volumes plus index), *https://rutlandhistory.com/new-hampshire-state-papers/*; 3) ancestry.com.

4. U.S. National Archives, *Register of Enlistments in the U.S. Army, 1798-1914*, M233, Records of the Adjutant General's Office, 1780s-1917, Record Group 94, "Manly H. Brown," accessed at *U.S. Army Register of Enlistments, 1798-1914*, ancestry.com.

5. *Bangor Whig and Courier*, 22 May 1891, page 3; accessed at newspapers.com.

6. U.S. National Archives, *U.S. War of 1812 Pension Files 1812-1815*, SO33271, "Thomas G. Brown," accessed at Fold3.com.

7. See Note 6.

8. "The Story of the Twenty-First Regiment, Connecticut Volunteer Infantry, During the Civil War 1861-1865," Members of the Regiment, Middletown, Conn., Press of the Stewart Printing Co., 1900 p355-356, digitized by *Google*.

9. U.S. National Archives, *Letters received by the Office of the Adjutant General, Main Series 1861-1870*, M619, Record Group 94, Roll 0240, 1864, B922 Conn., "Thomas G. Brown," accessed at Fold3.com.

10. Typed notes on members of the Brown Family, most likely from unsourced newspaper obituaries, author's personal collection.

Chapter 4

The Adventures of Ezra Jones, Laura's Grandfather

Breaching the Brick Wall

Laura Brown's mother, Mary Jones, and her Jones family presented a classic genealogical brick wall. Laura's birth record in Vermont Vital Records stated that her mother, Mary Jones, was born in what appears to be "Elmira. N.Y." This misinformation resulted in fruitless searches of Mary Joneses in central New York, the preponderance of whom were Irish servants. Focusing on the Lamoille County towns of Wolcott and Hyde Park, I contacted a local researcher who was able to view the Hyde Park town records and provide me with critical information. The marriage record of Mary and Ira Brown in Book D, p3 in Hyde Park Town Clerk's Office (now searchable online) stated Mary as the daughter of George and Ann Jones. Mary's parent's names on her second marriage record were Ezra C. and Ann Jones. How the name "George" came to be and what "C." represents are mysteries that have not been resolved. Decennial censuses and the birth records of their children showed that "Ann" was actually Chloe A. or Chloe Ann Haskins but her name has been documented as Ann, Flora, Claira, and Chlora. Various records show that Mary was born in "Maury" (likely Moira, N.Y., and probably where the confusion with Elmira came from) and Malone, N.Y., which is less than 15 miles from Moira, and may actually represent the same birth location.

Chloe's mother, Elsa Darling, was from the prominent Darling family that lived in Morristown before her father settled in nearby Elmore. Elsa died when Chloe was two years old. Chloe's father, Hiram C. Haskins, married again two years later to Charlotte Wright, but Charlotte died not long after their son Hiram Sereno Haskins was born. Hiram (Sr.) married a third time to Harriet Whitcomb with whom he had a son Adorno and a daughter Elizabeth (who died at eight years old).

However, the brick wall loomed even higher behind Ezra C. Jones. No birth record for Ezra had been found and after many frustrating and pointless searches using information reported on his death certificate, it was determined that the certificate contained erroneous information – his birth place was one of two states; and the birth date and name of his father were wrong! The informant, possibly his nephew who boarded with him in 1900, provided the name and birthdate of Ezra's next older brother, Nathaniel Jones, who was born in New York State to a different mother!

An in-depth search, prompted by DNA matching, a search in the Hyde Park library for any Joneses, and a newspaper announcement for a trial found in an on-line database, led to the heir search contained in a contested probate for Pauline Jones.[1] The probate confirmed that Ezra was a brother to Pauline, that they shared siblings, and that

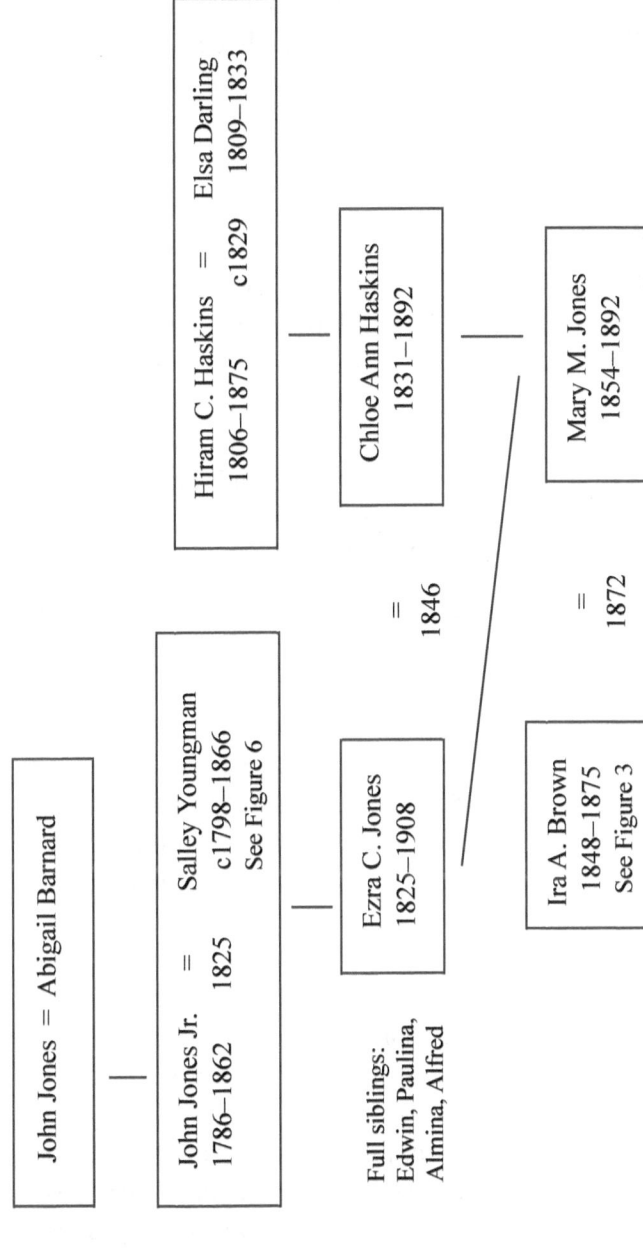

Figure 4. Line of Descent to Mary M. Jones.

Ezra's father was named John Jones not Nathaniel Jones. This discovery enabled further research to reveal that his mother was Salley Youngman, daughter of a Revolutionary War patriot.

Ezra's Early Years

Ezra C. Jones was most decidedly a "character," but certainly not a rambling man like his father John Jones. Except for a short time in Malone, N.Y. where second daughter Mary M. Jones (Laura Mary Brown's mother) was born in 1854, Ezra spent his adult life in Lamoille County, Vermont- mostly in Hyde Park, with a brief stay in Wolcott, and his final years in Garfield, formerly a village but now an area included in the town of Hyde Park.

John Jones was born in Goffstown, New Hampshire. As a young man he moved to Washington, Vt. where he married Margaret Nelson in 1806 and where two sons were born. The young family then moved on to Candor, N.Y. where two more sons and possibly some daughters were born. Margaret died circa 1824 and subsequently John moved back to Washington leaving a toddler son behind with John's sister in New York. In Washington, John married Salley Youngman and nine months later Ezra was born. Several more children were born in Washington and then around 1840 the Joneses moved north to Hyde Park, Vt. Less than ten years later, John packed up most of his family, minus the oldest and youngest sons, and moved to St. Lawrence County, N.Y. By the 1860 census the family was living in Hyde Park again. John Jones died in Morristown and his final resting place is unknown. Salley died in Hyde Park and lies in Holbrook Cemetery. Many of John Jones' descendants have lived in Lamoille County ever since.

Ezra, however, found Hyde Park to be home. He married local girl Chloe Haskins on the 28 October 1846 and a daughter was born in a reasonable time. Sometime after the 1850 census the young family made the trek west across northern New York to Franklin County where some of Chloe's mother's family, the Darlings, lived. On May 8, 1851 two letters were advertised as waiting for Ezra Jones at the Malone Post Office. Alice and Mary were born in the Bangor/Malone area in 1854. The New York sojourn was brief as Ezra bought land on Diggins Road, Hyde Park, in 1855. By the census of 1860 the Jones family included two more children, but had lost Alice. In 1863, Ezra registered for the Civil War listing Morristown, Vt. as his residence.

Ezra began a pattern of housing boys that were not his sons. When John Jones went off to upstate New York in the late 1840s, he either left the youngest son behind or sent him back to Vermont prior to 1850. Alfred, age 9, was living with his brother and wife, Ezra and Chloe, and their first child, Elsa, when the 1850 census was made in Hyde Park, Vt. Alfred was not listed with his parents in Lawrence, N.Y. Families struggling to make ends meet often sent children out of the family home, once they were old enough to be useful elsewhere. Farm work is rarely all done.

Franklin County is adjacent to St. Lawrence County and thus the towns of Lawrence and Malone, N.Y. are thirty miles apart on current Route 11. Moira and Bangor, towns found on daughter Mary's vital records, can be found along Route 11. When Ezra left Vermont for Franklin County, he likely took Alfred with him and returned him to their parents, John and Salley Jones.

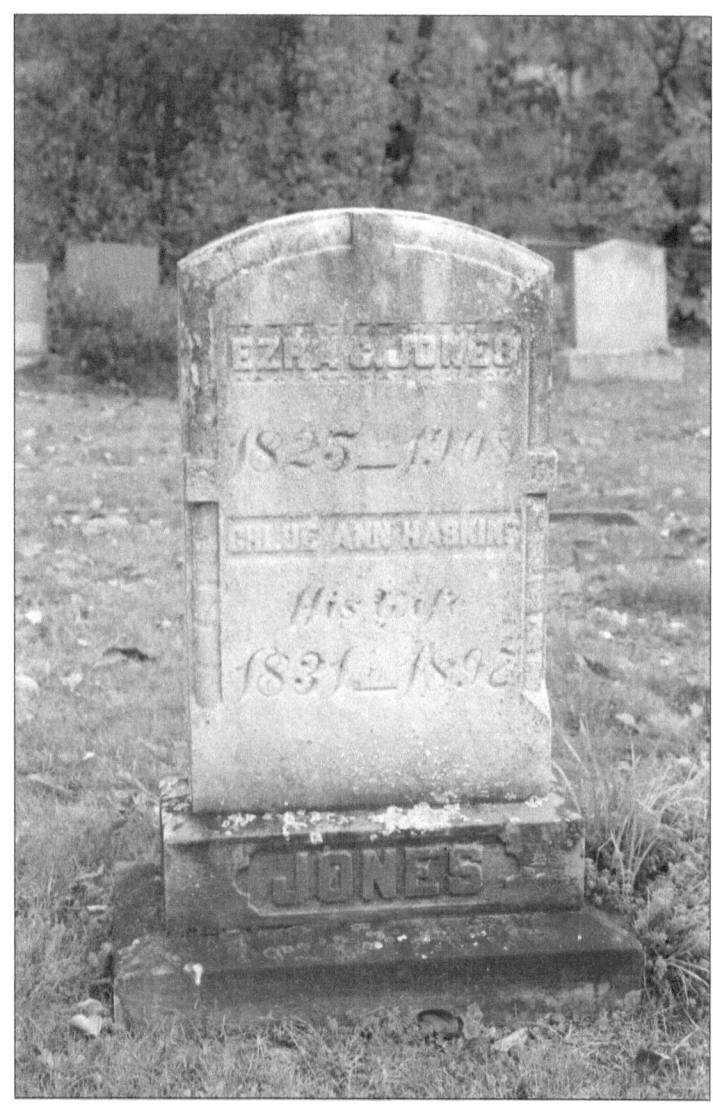

Shared headstone for Ezra C. Jones and Chloe Ann Haskins, Center Cemetery, Hyde Park, Vt. Photo by author.

Center Cemetery on McKinstry Hill, burial site of Ezra and Chloe Jones. Photo by author.

At the turn of the century, and after Chloe died, Ezra was living in Hyde Park in a dwelling he owned. Daughter Lillian and her family were enumerated separately but rented from Ezra. Ezra listed a 42-year-old, divorced man named Andrew Jones as a boarder. It seems Andrew was the son of Ezra's brother, Edwin, and was between marital relationships at the time.

Prior to this nephew, Ezra had housed boys that were not his own while living in Wolcott in 1880. Below the two youngest daughters Cora and Lillian, the census lists Eddie M. Jones, white male, age 12, born in Vermont, and Eddie Moors, age 10, also a white male born in Vermont. Who were their parents? Why were they living with the Joneses? How long did they stay? These questions remain as the mystery of the two Eddie's has yet to be solved.

Ezra in the News

Ezra Jones was most certainly comfortable in the hills and dales around Hyde Park, Vt. The Lamoille County business directory of 1883 lists Ezra as a farmer in Morrisville with a threshing machine. Morrisville was the village center of the town of Morristown. Farming was a common occupation for the Jones family members. In November of the same year, the *News and Citizen* column from North Wolcott reports: "Ezra Jones, with a one horse machine, threshed 83 bushels of oats for H. W. Camp in four and one-half hours. Who can beat it?"[2]

Published items suggest that Ezra periodically worked in the neighboring communities. Since 1873, Ezra and Chloe had lived and farmed on 45 acres described as part of the third division of Hyde Park but became the village of

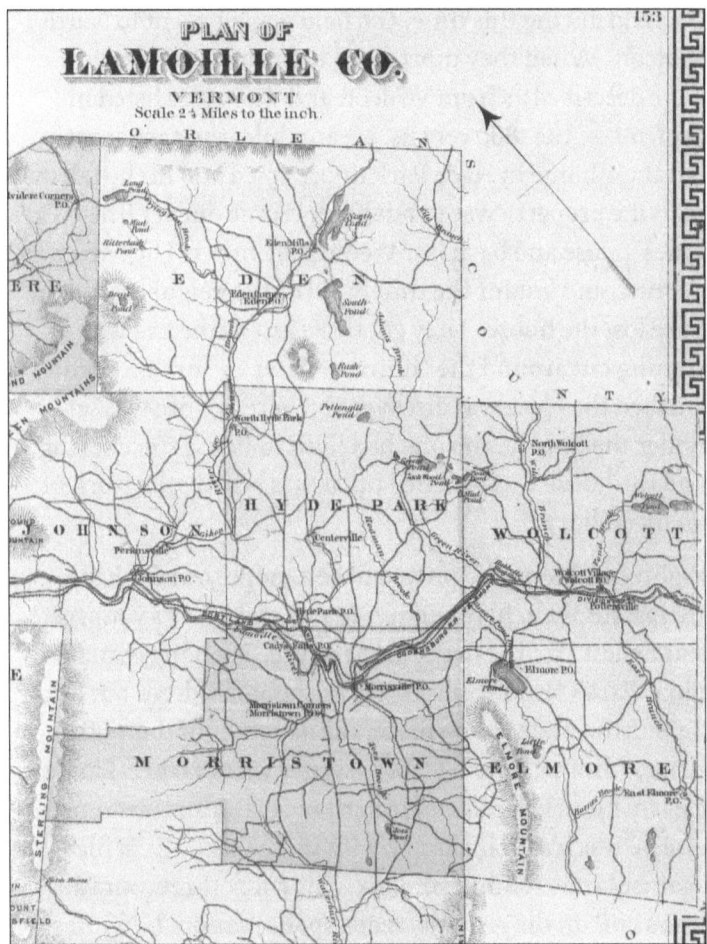

Map 4. Partial Plan of Lamoille Co., Vermont, 1876. Courtesy of David Rumsey Map Collection.

Garfield during this time. Garfield was adjacent to North Wolcott. When they mortgaged their farm in 1880 they were described as from Wolcott and they were listed in Wolcott on the 1880 census. Meanwhile, they apparently left their home in Hyde Park unoccupied and in the fall of 1886 the property was vandalized. "Some one set fire to Ezra Jones' house and barn last Wednesday night. The barn was burned, and but for the timely aid of the neighbors would have lost the house. They got there just as the fire was coming out around the chimney. After the fire was extinguished the place was discovered where the fire was set under the floor. As no one had lived in house since spring, and the house was fastened up, it was plainly the work of an incendiary."[3]

Eighteen ninety-two proved to be a tough year for Ezra. He lost his wife, his daughter Mary, and Mary's youngest son Ernest Darling to the circle of life. Then in February of 1894, Ezra's sister Pauline died without children, but left her entire estate to one niece, the daughter of their other sister, Almina, who had died twenty years earlier. Ezra was clearly knowledgeable of inheritance laws and customs or else he was just plain angry with niece Lizzie. Ezra filed suit against Lizzie P. Smith in 1894. The court threw out Pauline's will on the grounds that a spouse cannot be witness to a will even though the spouse will not inherit. This meant that Pauline's siblings or their offspring would inherit, and thus began a ten-year search for the heirs. In 1904, Pauline's estate of $748.11 was settled yielding $168.00 for distribution to her siblings and their heirs - 31 recipients. Ezra and his two living brothers received $21.00, Lizzie Smith received $1/32^{nd}$ or $5.25 as did all her cousins, and the smallest amount 1/215th ($0.77) went to 8 grandchildren

> ministrator has leave to enter to defend. Darling for plff. Hebard pro se.
> No. 395, Salmon B. Hebard, exr, of last will of Pauline A. Cabot, Lizzie P. Smith legatee v. Ezra Jones. Appeal from Probate. Death of plff. suggested. J. K. Darling adm. has leave to enter to prosecute. Darling for plff., Powers for deft.
> No. 400, Emma J. Cutler v. Syrena Clark.

"*Orange County Court, Dec. Term, 1894,*" United Opinion, 21 Dec 1894, col. 5.

> manded for assessment of damages.
> Salmon B. Hebard executor of last will of Pauline A. Cabot, Lizzie P. Smith, legatee, Apt., v. Ezra Jones.—An appeal from Probate from Orange County. The judgment that the instrument propounded as the last will and testament of Pauline Cabot was not her last will and testament was affirmed and ordered to be certified to Probate Court.
> Enos C. Fish v. Charles A. Thompson,

Vermont Watchman, 27 Nov 1895, p. 4.

Looking toward Diggins Road from McKinstry Hill Road, Hyde Park, Vt. Photo by author.

and great grandchildren of deceased siblings. Hopefully, Ezra was satisfied with the results, although I would imagine his relationship with Lizzie was severely jeopardized.[4]

In his final years, Uncle Ezra often visited friends or the children of his siblings in the Mc'Kinstry Hill area. McKinstry Hill Road heads north just after the Center Cemetery on Centerville Road. Lower Diggins Road turns north toward original lot 51 which was probably the first land that Ezra owned in Hyde Park-bought in 1855-and then sold to in 1859 and 1863 to Salmon Niles, later the first husband of Pauline Jones. For many years the Diggins area was the site of lumber and mill activity carried out by Chloe Jones' half-brother, Hiram Sereno Haskins, and was briefly called Haskinsville. The Mc'Kinstry column in the local paper often remarked on Ezra Jones. "Uncle Ezra Jones from Garfield visited friends here Friday." Two weeks later, "Ezra Jones from Garfield visited at Orvis Jones' last Sunday and Monday." And again, in August he makes the Mc'Kinstry Hill news: "Ezra Jones of Garfield, is visiting friends on the hill."[5]

The following news item merited printing in *The Barre Daily Times,* the *Herald and News,* and the *Middlebury Register* (1907):

> "Ezra Jones, aged 86, who lives near Green River, is recovering from one of the most harrowing experiences on record. The old gentleman was found hanging from a woven wire fence, a rope about his neck, and bleeding profusely from several wounds. The circumstances point to suicide, but Jones claims he was on his way cross lots and fell in an attempt to climb the fence, catching his feet in the upper interstice. As his cries brought no help and his suffering became unbearable, he tried to cut an artery

in his wrist and his throat. Not being successful, he tried to strangle himself with the rope but was too weak to accomplish his purpose."[6]

McKinstry Hill was located to the west of Garfield and the farm of Ezra. To get there today, one must circumvent the Green River Reservoir by driving southeast on Garfield Road to Cleveland Corners, turning right and following the Cleveland Corners Road west until you meet Center Road. There you turn right again on Center Road until you reach McKinstry Hill Road. This route is approximately 4.5 miles. Since Ezra's farm was located near the intersection of current Bornemann Road and Garfield Road, a huge obstacle at that time would have been the crossing of the Green River. Thus, the distance from his home in Garfield to his former haunt of McKinstry Hill was less than two miles as the crow flies – or as the old man travels. Surely, Ezra's unfortunate incident on the Green River surely started as a normal, well-traveled trek to or from McKinstry Hill.

On March 18, 1908 the *News and Citizen* reported the following in the Garfield section: "Ezra Jones, who has been ill for a long time, passed away Friday night. He spent his last days at the home of his daughter, Mrs. Sydney Bartlett. Funeral services were held at the house Sunday..." In the same column was a mention of Ezra's grandson, "Harold Bartlett, while splitting wood last Saturday, cut his foot so badly..."[7] Lillian Jones Bartlett most certainly had a rough week. Ezra was buried in Center Cemetery on Centerville Road with his wife of 40+ years.

Ezra, a Vibrant Character

Ezra was a versatile, independent, successful man. Family was important as shown by the numerous individuals who stayed in his home throughout the years and the cross-country trips to visit the Joneses on McKinstry Hill. The *News and Citizen* reported visits to cousin Alvah Jones and son Orvis.[8] Alvah was son of Ezra's next younger brother Edwin and married to Mary Jane Emerson.[9] Edwin's son, Andrew, boarded with his uncle Ezra in 1900. Descendants of Ezra's brother, Alfred Jones, the progenitor of Joneslan Farm in North Hyde Park, Vt., recall talk of "Uncle Ezra."

Sometime after 1868 when Ezra purchased lots 44 and 45 on Garfield Road, he passed the lots on to Ira Brown. As the widow of Ira, Mary Jones Brown received the land in probate in 1876 and then sold it by the end of the year. Ezra also acquired land on Hyde Park Plains that son Wilbur had owned, possibly helping him out of a financial problem. Ezra seems to have acquired and sold land profitably and took advantage of mortgage opportunities.

Besides being savvy in land transactions, Ezra was knowledgeable and determined enough to contest the will of his sister. In mid-life Pauline married a widower, Salmon Niles, whom Ezra had sold property to over the years. Salmon dropped dead the morning after his wedding to Pauline. Several years later she married Hyde Cabot. Pauline certainly acquired money from her years of employment but whether she inherited from the Jones parents or from Salmon Niles, Ezra clearly felt her estate belonged elsewhere in the family rather than to only one niece.

In a twist of versatility, Ezra and Chloe leased a sawmill operation in 1864 for five years in the Cadys Falls area

View of Cadys Falls, Vt. Photo by author.

Remnants of a mill at Cadys Falls, Vt. Photo by author.

of Hyde Park. The premises included a mill dam, floom (now known as flume), water rights, and land for storing lumber. Chloe's half-brother Hiram Sereno Haskins, was a "mill man" and owned land on Lower Diggins. The Joneses may have been encouraged or assisted by Haskins. However, Ezra's tenacity was put to the test toward the end of the lease. On 18 January 1870, the following appeared in the Hyde Park *Lamoille Newsdealer*:

> *State's Attorney Bingham brought up Mr. Curtis Eastman last week, for an assault on Ezra C. Jones, and after an all night trial the court fined Eastman $10 and costs. Eastman undertook to drive Ezra away from a spring where he had been in the habit of getting water, –using an axe as a persuader, and Ezra defended himself with a scythe. No blood was shed.*[10]

Since Ezra was a successful wheat farmer and fast harvester, it is not surprising that he was skilled with a scythe and capable of using it in a defensive maneuver. After this event, Ezra returned to farming.

Endnotes

1. The journey to discover the parents and family of Ezra C. Jones can be read in: Priscilla L. Partridge, "The Lost Siblings of Ezra C. Jones of Hyde Park, Vermont," *Vermont Genealogy* (Vol. 21, No. 1, Spring 2016).

2. "North Wolcott," *(Morrisville) News & Citizen,* 8 Nov. 1883, col. 5.

3. "North-east Ripples," *(Morrisville) News & Citizen,* 28 Oct. 1886, p. 3.

4. See note 1.

5. "Mc'Kinstry Hill," *(Morrisville and Hyde Park) News and Citizen:* 1 March 1905, p. 4; 15 March 1905, p. 4; 16 Aug. 1905, p. 4.

6. "About the State," *(Barre, Vt.) The Barre Daily Times,* 27 Aug. 1907, p. 7, col. 4; "Late State News," *(West Randolph, Vt.) Herald and News,* 29 Aug. 1907, p. 2, col. 5; "State News," *(Middlebury, Vt.) Middlebury Register,* 30 Aug.1907, p. 3, col. 3.

7. "Garfield," *(Morrisville and Hyde Park) News and Citizen,* 18 March 1908, p. 4.

8. "Mc'Kinstry Hill," *(Morrisville and Hyde Park) News and Citizen,* 15 March 1905, p. 4.

9. Mary Jane Jones' mother was a pauper in Eden, Vt. Mary Jane and Abigail's story can be read in Karl Lamson, "Abigail Goodenough, A Pauper of Eden, Vermont," *Vermont Genealogy* (Vol. 23, no. 2, Fall 2018).

10. "No. Hyde Park," *(Hyde Park, Vt.) Lamoille Newsdealer,* 18 Jan. 1870, p. 2, col. 2.

Chapter 5
The Sally Vignettes... Fowler-Davis-Banfill

Sally Fowler and her granddaughter Sally Banfill

In November 2016, a girl was born in California. Her parents named her Sally - the first Sally in generations. Unbeknownst to her parents, the baby descends from numerous Sallys, ancestors of her great grandmother Miriam, and all were pioneer women of New England.

Three Sallys - Salley Youngman, Sally Banfill, and Sally Safford - were of the same generation back from young Sally (the 8th) whereas Sally Kettell, Sally Fowler, her mother Sarah Flanders and her grandmother Sarah Prince were part of the 9th-12th generations. Sally (Banfill) Davis and Salley (Youngman) Jones became grandmothers-in-law in 1872 when their grandchildren Ira A. Brown and Mary M. Jones married.

The name "Sally" was often used as a nickname for Sarah during the 18th century in New England and earlier in Europe and this was the case in these families. The women discussed here were known by either name at various times in their lives. Many of these Sallys, antecedents of Miriam Ingalls and young Sally, lived in remote, mountainous areas with scattered populations. Sally Safford lived in the outskirts of Boston, Mass. and may have had a slightly more "urban" lifestyle than the others. She was certainly exposed to the tumultuous end of the British Colonial rule. In addition to living lives as pioneers and farmers, all were daughters, sisters, or wives of Revolutionary War or War of 1812 patriots.

Sally Fowler 1742–1817

Sarah "Sally" Fowler was the third of four generations of Sarah. It is not surprising that a nickname might be used to distinguish her from her mother Sarah Flanders, although later records show that she went by Sarah. Sarah was born in 1742 in coastal New Hampshire, in the town of South Hampton. Her parents, Abner and Sarah (Flanders) Fowler, were married in Salisbury, Essex County, Mass., where they were born and raised, but had relocated by the time of Sarah's birth. It appears that Abner (Sr.) moved his family again to the wilds of Orange County, Vermont before his death in Newbury, Vt. although no headstone or death record has been found. He, or his son Abner, may have been a surveyor for the new town of Corinth.

Before settling permanently in Newbury, Abner and his family stopped off for a time in the area currently known as Concord, N.H. but was originally called Rumford. Between 1734 and 1765, the town of Rumford and the town of Bow N.H. squabbled over boundaries which resulted in unclear government and no recordkeeping. Hence basic information for this period and place is lacking. However, here, seventeen-year old Sarah Fowler reportedly married Ezekiel Colby and gave birth to six children including Miriam Colby (author's ancestor) and Sarah "Sally" Colby, the fourth Sally in that line. Ezekiel Colby's family was from the town of Amesbury, Mass. which lies across the Merrimack River from Newbury, Mass. and is adjacent to Salisbury, Mass. Possibly as early as 1772, Ezekiel and Sarah Colby had moved to the new town of Corinth-where six more children were born.

Zadock Thompson in his *A Gazetteer of the state of Vermont* presents a dramatic story that Ezekiel Colby and two other men went on a venture from Newbury (Vt.) to Corinth to collect maple syrup and that they were the first in that town.[1] However, the *History of Corinth* points out that the first charter for the town of Corinth was issued by Gov. Wentworth in 1764 and folks were known to have settled in the town at various times prior to 1772.[2]

Two Fowler men, probably Sarah's brothers Abner and Jacob, were recorded on the Payroll of Capt. Thomas' Company of Minute Men in Newbury for the year of 1776.[3] Her husband, Ezekiel Colby Sr., served as Captain of the Scouts for the town of Corinth during the Revolutionary War whereas Ezekiel Colby Jr. served in a militia. Both father and son have been honored for patriot service by the DAR.

Sarah Colby outlived her husband by twenty-six years. When Capt. Ezekiel Colby died, his wife was administrator of his estate. Sarah determined the estate to be insolvent so she turned over administration to a committee. The committee undertook an inventory and determined that the largest part of the debt was 21 pounds 2 shillings 9 pence

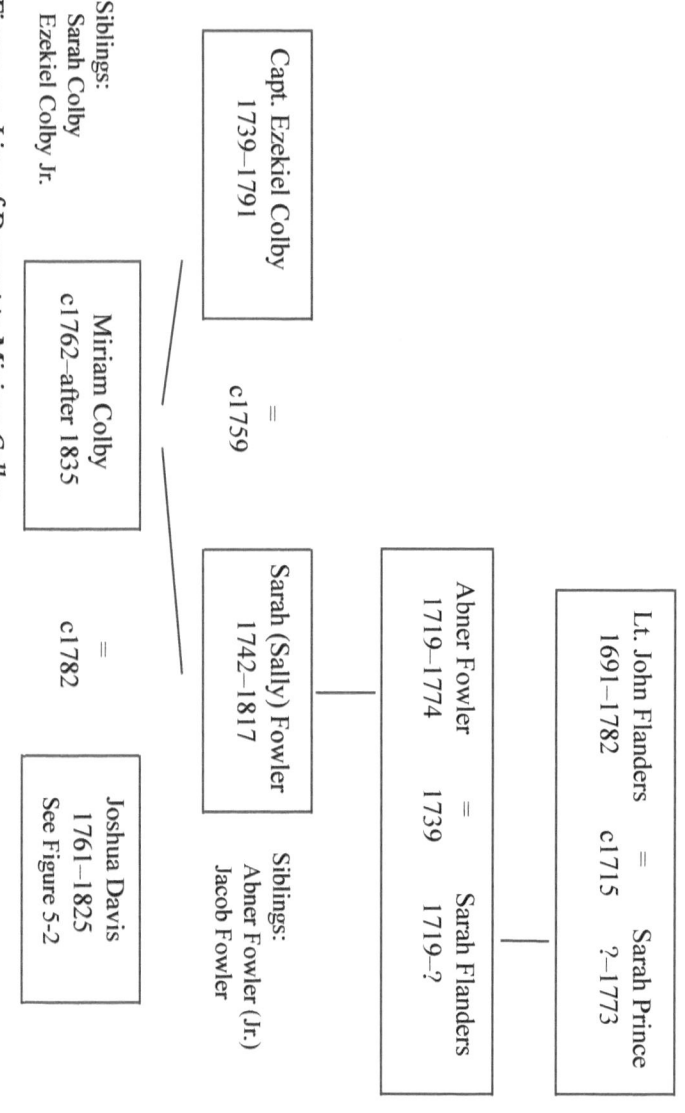

Figure 5-1. Line of Descent to Miriam Colby.

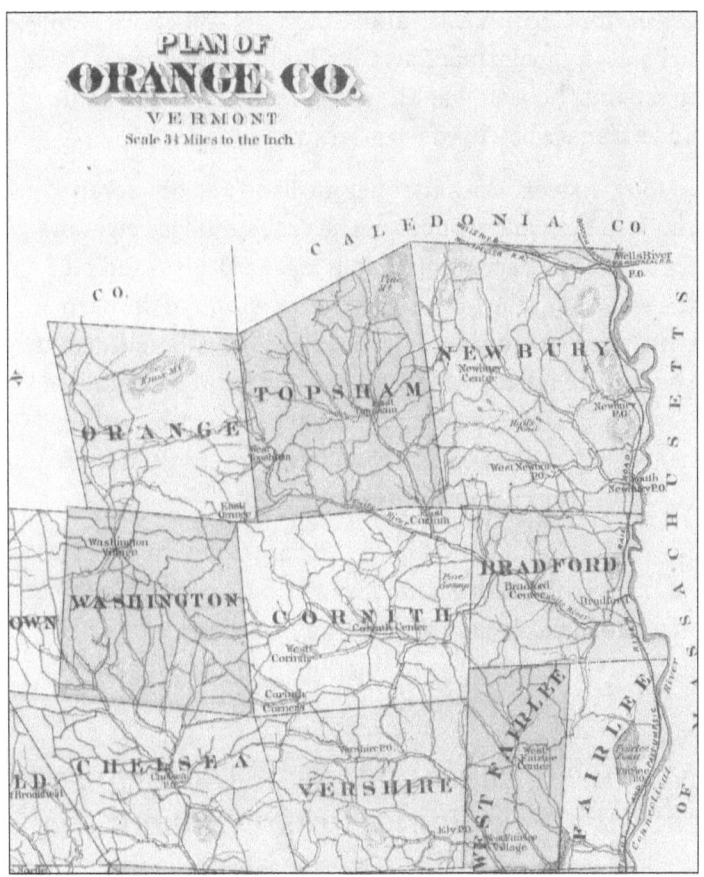

Map 5-1. Partial Plan of Orange Co., Vermont, 1876. Courtesy of David Rumsey Map Collection.

owed to her son-in-law, Joshua Davis. Sarah was ordered to sell enough land to satisfy that debt, which amounted to 40 acres and was documented on January 5, 1773. The 1800 census for Corinth lists Sarah Colby, her son Ezekiel Colby, her son-in-law Joshua Davis and his brother Simeon Davis in separate households. However, several younger adults and a teenage boy lived with Sarah.

In 1807, sixteen years after her husband's death, Sarah received her widow's dower. The probate judged awarded Sarah Colby 27 acres adjacent to Joshua Davis's land plus the east end of the house with the exception of the barn, which had already been given to her son Nathan. Current law required that a widow receive a share of the deceased husband's estate for the duration of her life. This ruling helped to prevent the care of widows and children from becoming the responsibility of the town.

Sarah and Ezekiel's first born, Miriam Colby, married Joshua Davis in Corinth about 1782. Miriam's brother Ezekiel married Joshua's sister Ruth Davis. Miriam Colby would become the 3rd great grandmother of Miriam Ingalls.

Northwest migration: from Massachusetts through New Hampshire to Vermont

The Fowler, Colby, and Davis families most likely knew each other prior to their settlement in Vermont. A common migration pattern for many folks living in coastal Colonial Massachusetts was to move slightly west and across the Merrimack River to Amesbury and Haverhill. From there, people went north to Hampton, New Hampshire or bought land in Kingstown (Kingston). Land ownership in Kingston became problematic as the states of New Hampshire

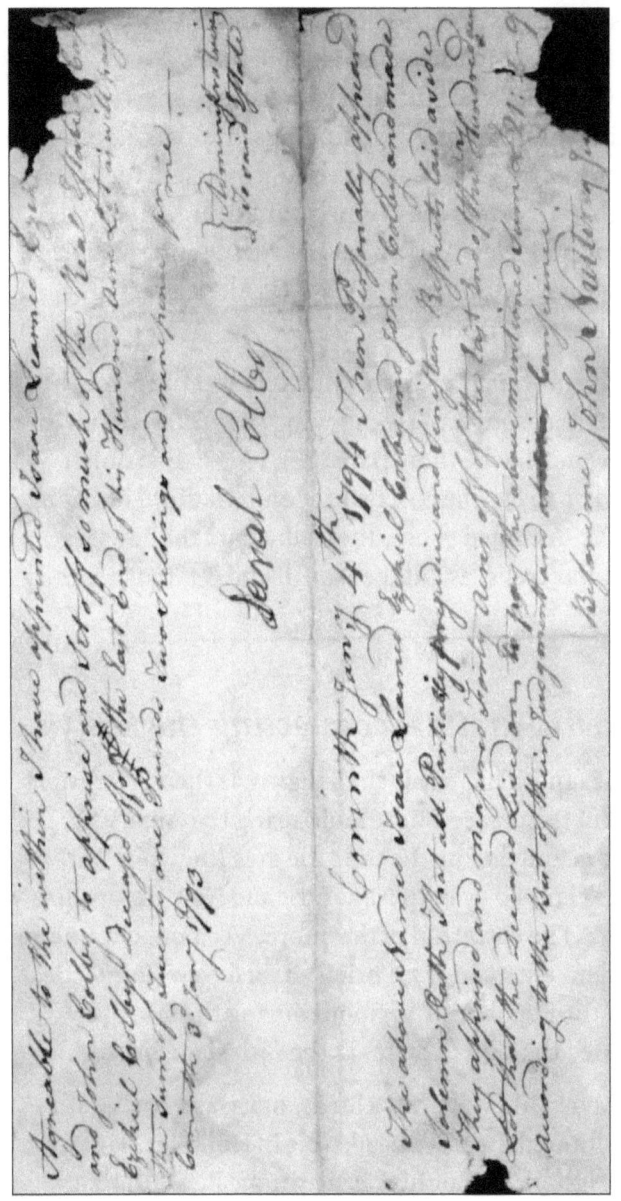

Sarah Colby's signature in her husband's probate documents, 1793.[4]

and Massachusetts disagreed on the boundary for a time. This was resolved in the 1740s. Then Benning Wentworth became Governor and encouraged westward movement by creating numerous new plantations or towns across New Hampshire. Some folks even continued further west and northward across the Connecticut River to the lands claimed by both New York State and New Hampshire. Settlers with New Hampshire Land Grant titles established the Republic of Vermont in 1777.

Most likely, Joshua Davis's parents followed this westward path from Amesbury, Mass.; moving slightly north up to Kingston and Hawke (now Danville), N.H.; then north westward up to Newbury, Corinth, and Bradford in Orange County, Vt. As noted above, the Colbys and the Fowlers made similar treks, as did the Banfill and Dearborn family members.

The Davis Family – connecting the Sallys

The Davis family history is challenging as their relocation to Vermont took place before and during the American Revolution, and during the time the area known as Vermont was claimed by both New York and New Hampshire and called "The Grants." Furthermore, Vermont became an independent entity in 1777; briefly called New Connecticut and then the Republic of Vermont during the War. Vermont joined the United States as the 14th state in 1791.

Joshua Davis's life story lacks birth, marriage, and death records although he has a headstone in Holland, New York, where he is honored for his service in the Revolutionary War by a monument adjacent to his burial in Humphrey Cemetery. In September of 1782 Joshua was a lieutenant under Captain Fish in the First Regiment of Militia which was tasked with assisting the sheriff in carrying out the laws. His brother Simeon also served in that unit.

The ancestry of Joshua Davis is subject to correlations, interpretations, and reliance on published genealogies, however, the proximity of Samuel and Dorothy Davis and their known son, David, in Corinth and Bradford supports the notion that Samuel and Dorothy Davis were Joshua's parents. The births of Joshua and Miriam's children were recorded in Corinth beginning in 1784. The naming pattern of Joshua and Miriam's children is telling: Their first son was named Ezekiel (after Miriam's father) and the second son Samuel (after Joshua's father). The first daughter was named Sarah (after Miriam's mother) and the second was Dolly (a nickname for Dorothy, Joshua's mother).

Although the first charters for Corinth exist, the early records of the towns settling were lost in a fire. Samuel, David, and Joshua do appear on a myriad of records in Corinth and Bradford beginning with statehood in 1791. A map of Corinth, created by James Whitelaw in 1790, shows the names of residents that were counted on the first census. Lot 24 is along the Bradford town line and shows "S. Davis pitched 1777" at the top and "J. Davis" in the center of the lot. We can only assume that "pitched" means that a person put up some kind of shelter on that land. Whether or not the squatter had permission from the land owner, is not known, but, often the landowners were speculators and needed someone to develop the property.

The 1764 plantation charter with New Hampshire set out conditions for the original grantees to follow to maintain their ownership. White and other pines were reserved for use as masts for the Royal Navy. Land owners had to plant

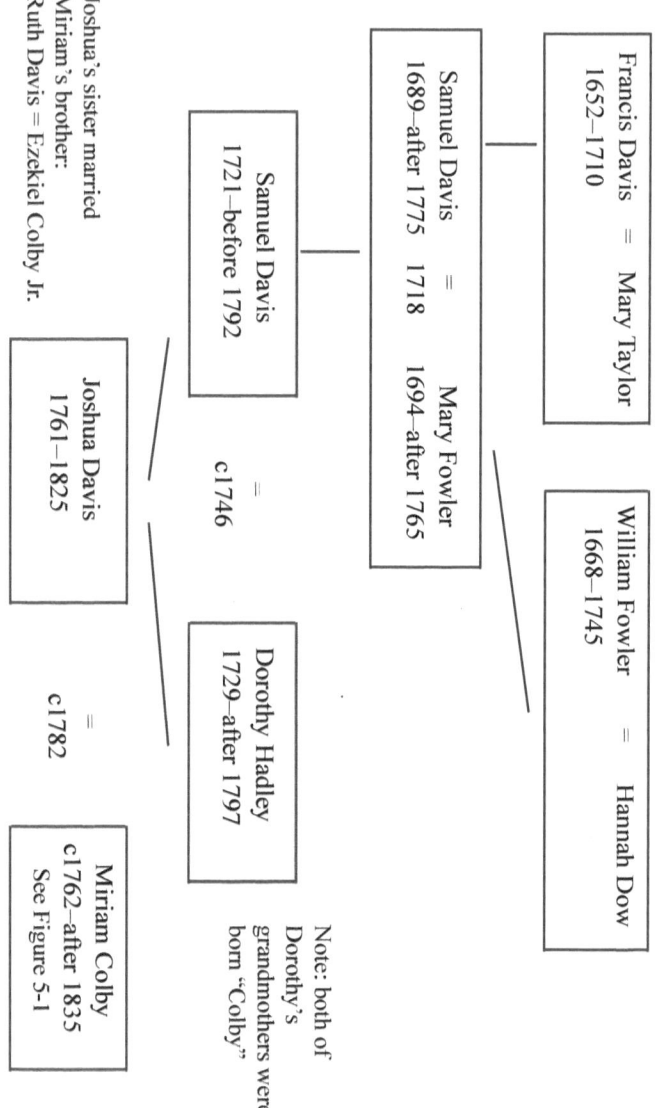

Figure 5-2 Line of Descent to Joshua Davis.

and cultivate 5 acres per each 50 acres within five years and pay an annual rent of one ear of Indian corn for ten years to the New Hampshire government. The New York charter (1772) required the planting and cultivation of 3 acres per 50 within three years. After 1774, a cash amount per 100 acres was to be paid by the owner, settler, or inhabitant of the land. Fortunately for the Davises, the borders of lot 24 were not affected by the differing surveys created for each charter.[5]

In the town of Corinth, landowners were not the only ones who paid taxes and could vote. Non-landowners or inhabitants, like Samuel, David, and Joshua Davis were freeman who were assessed taxes and allowed to vote. Hence, in 1783, their names can be found on a tax list where they were assessed 10 shillings. After many years in the area, Samuel Davis and David Davis each signed deeds for land in Corinth in 1788. David's property and residence were mentioned in Samuel's deed. In 1791, Joshua, at age thirty, purchased 100 acres of lot 24 where the family had been living for years. Meanwhile, Samuel had already purchased land in Bradford closer to and along the Connecticut River, which he then sold to David in 1790. Samuel and Dorothy were likely living in David's household in 1790.

Looking farther back, Joshua's father, Samuel Davis (Jr.), was born in Amesbury, Mass. and married Dorothy Hadley in Kingston, N.H. where the births of son David and daughters Mary and Judith were recorded. Unconfirmed sources suggest Joshua was born in Hawke which was a section of Kingston at that time. In 1760, Samuel Davis along with other Kingston men signed a petition to oppose the separation of land from Kingston to form Hawke; thus supporting Joshua's birth place as Hawke/Kingston. Land

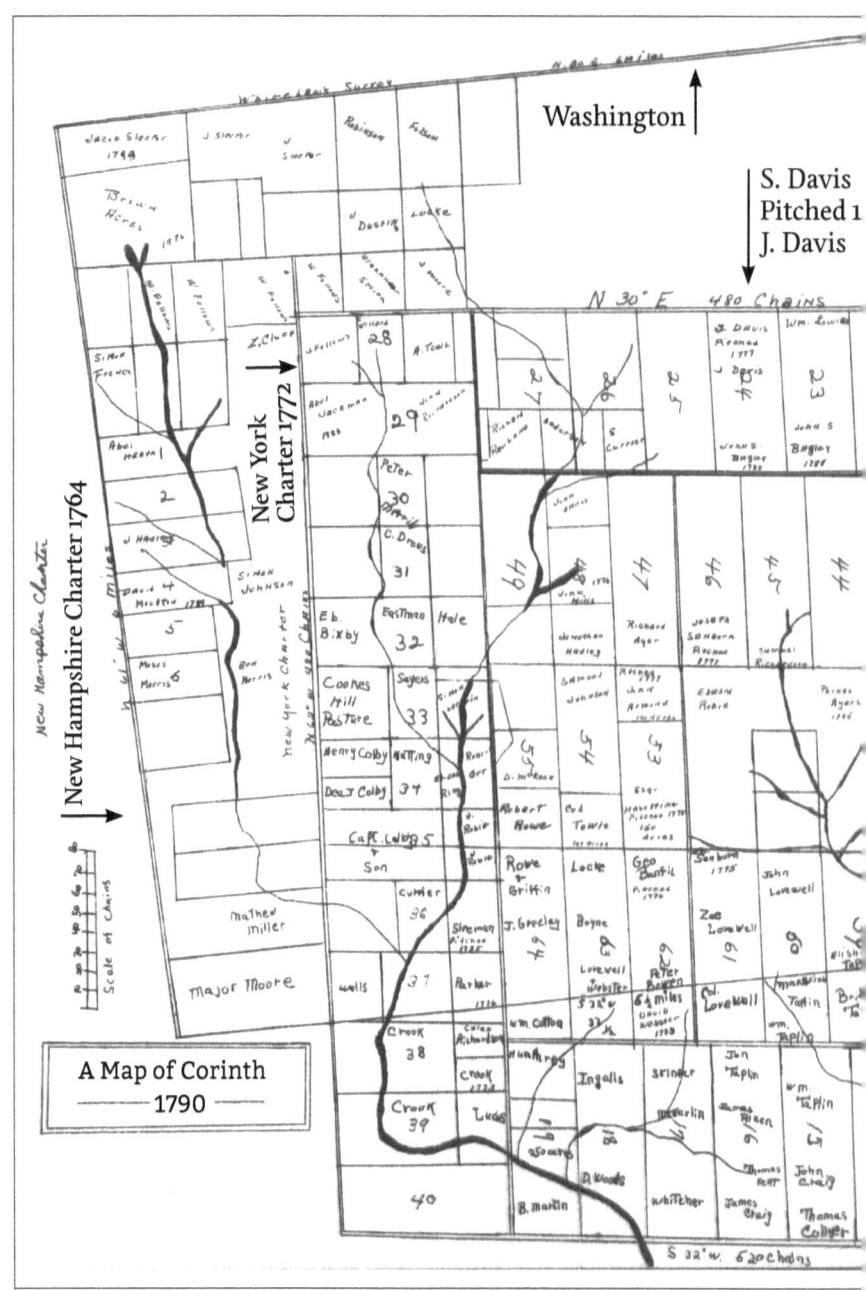

The Sally Vignettes...Fowler-Davis-Banfill

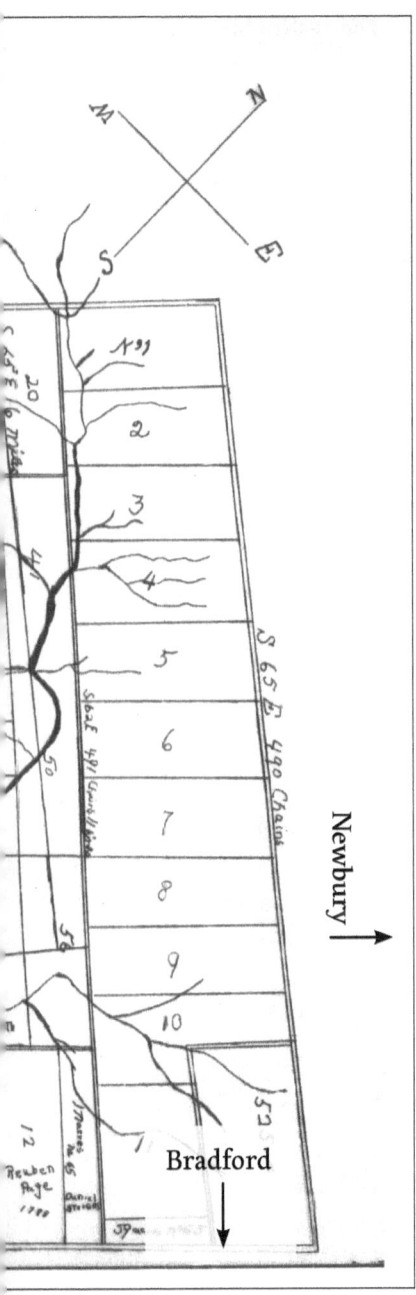

Map 5-2. Adapted map of Corinth, Vt. by James Whitelaw, 1790. From the History of Corinth (1995); courtesy of the Town of Corinth, Vt.

records show that Samuel (Jr.) sold off his Kingston land in the 1760s, shortly after the petition and separation. Birth records for more of Samuel and Dorothy's children begin in Corinth in 1767. Samuel, along with Abner Fowler (Jr.) and other men from Newbury, joined Capt. Bayley's Company in Col. Marsh's Regiment in September 1777 and served 51 days.

Samuel's parents, Samuel Davis (Sr.) and Mary Fowler, were born and married in Amesbury in 1718. Not long after his marriage, Samuel and his father-in-law, William Fowler, purchased land in Kingston, N.H., the first step in the northwestward migration. Samuel Sr. also sold his land in N.H. in the 1760s presumably to go west with his son and family. The time and place of Samuel's death is not known, but the deeds of his land in Kingstown were recorded in 1777. The last record of Mary Fowler Davis was her signature on those deeds in 1765.

Sally Banfill 1792–1876

Joshua and Miriam Davis's son, Nathan Davis, connects us to the another of the pioneer Sallys. Nathan married fellow Corinthian, Sally Banfill, in 1809. Sally's father, John, was the 5th generation of New Hampshire residents beginning with the earliest settler, John Banfill, who was born in either England or Barbados. John was a fisherman and mariner and settled in the Strawberry Banke area of Portsmouth, N.H. during the 1670s. Currently Strawberry Banke thrives as an historic waterfront neighborhood that highlights its history from Indigenous peoples to the present using costumed role players, demonstrations, buildings and gardens. The eldest, Hugh and at least seven more

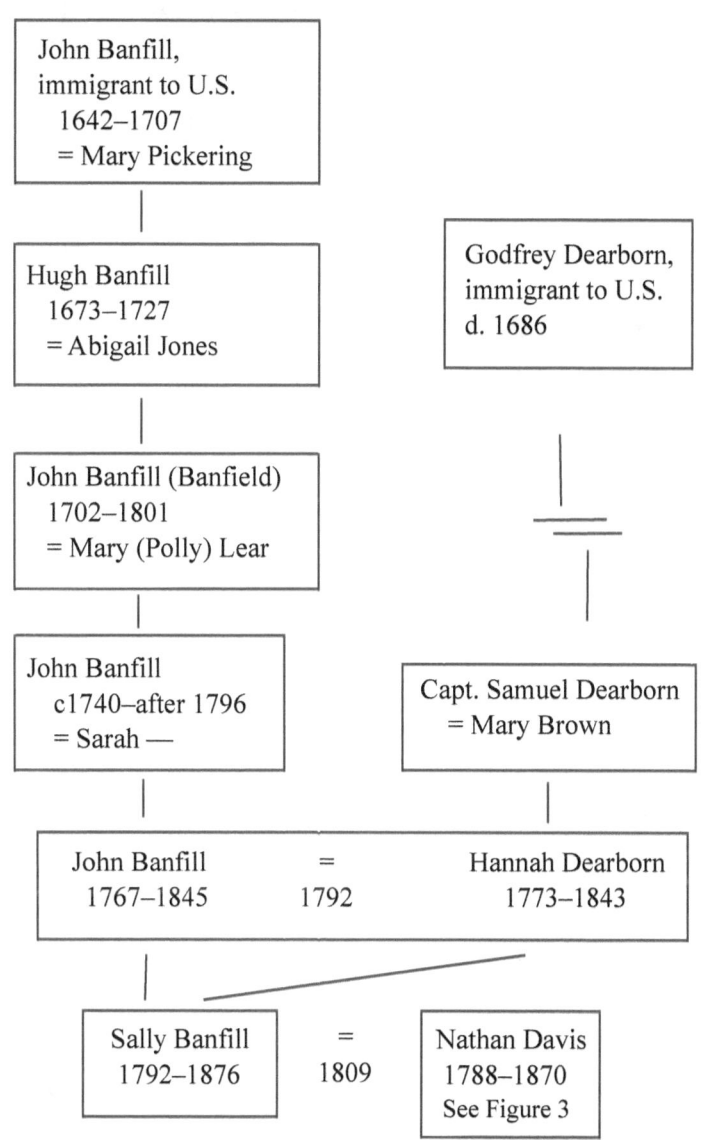

Figure 5-3. Line of Descent to Sally Banfill.

Banfill children were born in Portsmouth to the immigrant and his wife Mary. Hugh's son John married Mary (Polly) Lear of the well-known Portsmouth Lear family. Their son John (Jr.) and his family moved from Portsmouth, slightly to the west, to Nottingham where they raised their family.[6]

Sometime after the 1790 census was taken, John Banfill (Jr.) and his wife Sarah -, moved further west to Bradford, Vt., where Sarah outlived him. At about the same time, their son John Banfill (3rd) also relocated to Vermont after his marriage to Hannah Dearborn on 18 March 1792 in Nottingham, N.H. John and Hannah recorded the birth of their first child, daughter Sally Banfill, in Corinth on 26 June 1792. Both John (3rd) and Hannah Banfill are buried in Corinth Center Cemetery.

Hannah (Dearborn) Banfill descends from the well-known Rockingham County, N. H. family of Godfrey Dearborn.[7] Hannah's father, Captain Samuel Dearborn, and her mother, Mary (Brown) Dearborn, are also buried in Corinth Center Cemetery. Captain Dearborn enlisted from Epping, N.H. and served under Col. Stephen Peabody during the American Revolution.

Not long after Nathan Davis and Sally Banfill married in 1809, Nathan's brothers, his uncle Ezekiel Colby, and his Colby cousins began buying land in western New York from the Holland Land Company. As the Davises were farmers, and the terrain of Corinth was rocky and hilly with many trees, the advertisements for cheap land with improvements provided by the land company must have been enticing to these pioneering families. The lower cost of these lands also encouraged people to participate in businesses and occupations outside of farming.

Corinth Historical Society housed in the former Corinth Academy. Photo by author.

Building adjacent to Corinth Center Cemetery. Photo by author.

View across Corinth Center Cemetery including headstones of Capt. Samuel Dearborn and Mrs. Mary. Photo by author.

Nathan also contracted for land in New York after he served in the War of 1812. By 1824, Nathan's parents, Joshua and "Mary" Davis, had also purchased land in the frontier town of Holland, Erie County, N.Y. where Joshua died in 1825. It appears that Miriam Davis, who went by Mary on the Holland Land Company records, held on to their two 50 acre lots until 1835.

But, Nathan and Sally did not spend more than a few years in New York, and were back in Corinth by 1820 where they lived through 1840. Nathan continued his livelihood as a farmer after they moved north to Wolcott in Lamoille County. Insanity was reported as Nathan's cause of death whereas Sally died of old age six years after her husband. Nathan and Sally Davis were buried together in Fairmount Cemetery in Wolcott, Vt. Their partnership lasted six decades.

The year after Nathan and Sally's daughter, Philinda, married into the Brown family of Corinth, she and her new husband moved to Wolcott, likely the inspiration for her parents' relocation. Harvey and Philinda's son, Ira A. Brown, would marry into the Jones family of Hyde Park, thus connecting to another of the Sallys-Salley Youngman.

End Notes

1. Zadock Thompson, A. B., *A Gazetteer of the state of Vermont; containing A Brief General View of the State, A Historical and Topographical Description of the Counties, Towns, Rivers etc. Together with a Map and Several Engravings*, (Montpelier: E.P. Walton and the Author, 1824), p108.

2. Town of Corinth History Committee, *History of Corinth, Vermont 1764-1964*, (Corinth, Vt.: Town of Corinth, 1995). This book is an excellent resource for the early years of settlement. Town and land records can be found in Corinth and online at Family History Centers.

3. U.S. National Archives, *U.S. Revolutionary War Rolls, 1775-1783, Vermont*, Olcott's Regiment 1777-1781 folder 67, Various organizations folder 119, "Jacob Fowler" and "Abner Fowler," accessed at ancestry.com.

4. Probate of Ezekiel Colby, Bradford (Vt.) District Estate Files, Probate Records, Box 74106 1780-1800, FSL#004397760 img313, Familysearch.org.

5. See note 2. Correspondence with The Chair of the Selectboard, Corinth, reported that the map was not under copyright of the Town (May 6, 2025). A pdf of the Whitelaw map used in the *History of Corinth* was shared by the Town Historian.

6. Sybil Noyes, Charles Thornton Libby and Walter Goodwin Davis, *Genealogical Dictionary of Maine and New Hampshire* (Boston: New England Historic Genealogical Society, 1928-1939).

7. Joseph Dow, *The Dearborns of Hampton, N.H.; descendants of Godfrey Dearborn of Exeter and Hampton* (Salem: Salem Press Publishing and Printing Co., 1893).

Chapter 6
The Sally Vignettes... Youngman and Jones

Salley Youngman 1798-1866

Salley's name is spelled "S A L L E Y" on her headstone in Holbrook Cemetery, Hyde Park, Vt., so we will honor that. Salley Youngman was the daughter and grand-daughter of Revolutionary War heroes, Thomas and Nicholas Youngman. Nicholas remained in the town where he raised his children. In contrast, Thomas and his family experienced a more transient and nomadic life.

A New Hampshire Family in the Revolution – Nicholas Youngman and His Sons

Nicholas Youngman settled on One Pine Hill, originally under the governance of Dunstable, New Hampshire. Since the town and church were a considerable distance from his home, Nicholas was active in changing the jurisdiction of his home and land situated in West Dunstable to the closer town of Hollis, N.H. Nicholas' home still stands on Wheeler Road.

Nicholas Youngman, his five sons, and his three daughter's husbands, all from Hollis, fought in various capacities for the independence of the American Colonies from Britain. Nicholas and son John served together in July of 1776 on the expedition to Ticonderoga. Ebenezer responded to the Lexington Alarm on April 19, 1775 with other men from Hollis. Ebenezer then joined a Massachusetts company and proceeded to Cambridge where he died during the battle at Bunker Hill on 17 June 1775. John and Thomas enlisted together for three years from 1777–1780. Muster rolls show that both were sick at different times while at Valley Forge. Thomas re-enlisted in 1782 for a brief time. John appears to have served most of the war in Capt. Fry's Co. In 1782, Jabez and Stephen enlisted together and served in Col. Dearborn's Regiment.

Of the sons-in-law, Simeon Blood was a private in Capt. McNalley's Co. of Col. Joseph Cilley's 1st Regiment. David Sherer was also a private in Col. Cilley's Regiment under Capt. Nathaniel Hutchins. Joseph French enlisted in the company of Capt. Towne of Amherst and later joined the 27th Massachusetts Regiment at the siege of Boston.

After the war, John Youngman married and settled in Barnet, Vermont, where he and wife Abigail had four children baptized in the Presbyterian Church. The records show that John had a contentious relationship with the Church. It seems likely that he suffered from post-traumatic stress disorder. In 1811, life estate was set up in Barnet for John and his wife dependent on good behavior, but what happened to them after that has not been determined. John likely died before the pension act was created. John's daughter, Mary, was married in 1815 in Stanbridge (Dunham), Quebec, which is north across the Canadian border from Highgate,

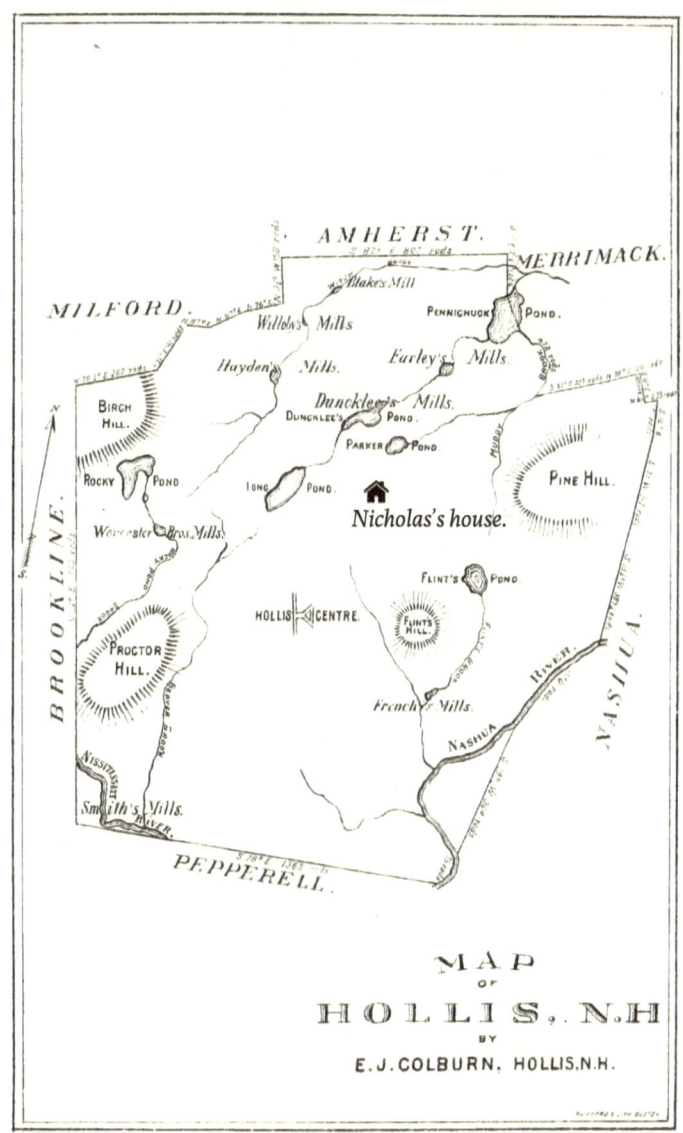

Map 6-1. Adaptation of E. J. Colburn map of Hollis, N.H. showing Pine Hill. The town of Nashua on the right side border was originally the town of Dunstable. (Samuel T. Worcester, History of the Town of Hollis, N.H.)

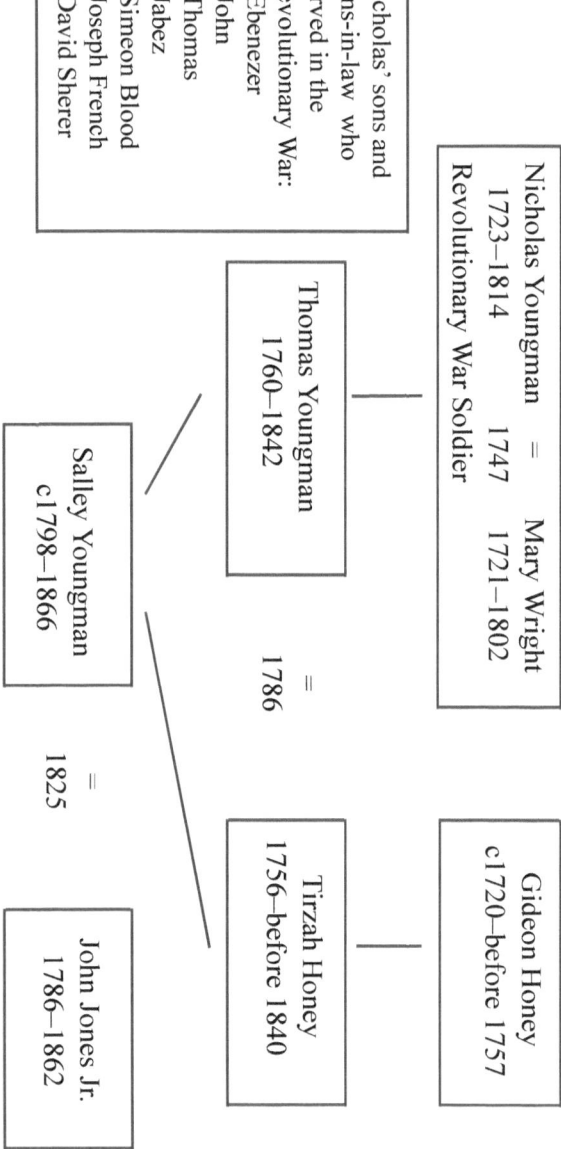

Figure 6. Line of Descent to Salley Youngman.

Vt. Some family trees suggest John died in Stanstead, Quebec which lies north of Barnet.

Salley's Father, Thomas Youngman

Salley's father, however, did live long enough to apply for a Revolutionary War pension on 4 April 1818. The application contains Thomas's recollections of the battles and places he served during his three-year enlistment: the march to Ticonderoga, the Battle of Stillwater, the taking of Burgoyne. Pension documents show that he was a private in Scammel's Regiment of the New Hampshire Line. He stated that he was "now old super annuated ... and poor to the last degree." In 1820, Thomas was required to appear before the Court to confirm his enlistment. He reported his age as 58, having a few animals and household items, and that his "family consists of myself poor & needy not able to work much my wife Tirzah aged 54 years not able to do much hard work." Thomas received a pension of $8 per month until his death 1 October 1842 in Morristown, Vt.[1]

After Thomas' service in the War, he married Tirzah Honey in Hollis, N.H. in November of 1786 but moved on to Barnet, Vt. where his brother John was living. In 1790 and 1791, Thomas was co-owner of a pew in the Barnet Presbyterian Church. Thomas and Tirzah may have moved to Barnet as early as June of 1787. The town records note that on 6 June 1787 the constable was directed to warn "Lucretia Youngman as a transient person" to leave Barnet with her effects within 20 days.[2] "Warning out" of newcomers was a practice of New England communities to protect the town from having to assume the physical care and cost of impoverished individuals, particularly, those newly arrived in town. Vermont no longer allowed this practice after 1817.

Since this warning out took place in 1787, seven months after Thomas' marriage to Tirzah, it seems likely that "Lucretia" was actually Tirzah Youngman and that her residency was established within the 20 days as required by the warning. Although both John and Jabez lived in Barnet and owned land there, Jabez's wife, Susannah already had a child, so that she would have been warned with her child or family. The first known child of John and his wife, Abigail, was not born until 1790. They were probably married circa 1788 or 1789, after the warning out event was recorded.

Thomas and Tirzah moved north and westward to Highgate, Vt. where they lived from 1795 to at least 1804. Thomas and Tirzah had three known daughters-Betsey (b. 1789), Lucinda (b. 1797), and Salley (b. 1798). These girls are confirmed by the 1800 census. It is believed that Thomas then moved to Canada for a few years. Daughter Salley may have been the "Sarah" Youngman who served as witness to a baptism in St. Armand, Brome, Quebec in 1815. Eldest daughter Betsey (Elizabeth) married during this time and records show that her first child, Thomas Whitcomb, was born in Dunham, Quebec in 1811.

At this time, the part of the North American continent that lay between the St. Lawrence River and the American border was called the Eastern Townships of Quebec. The area had been organized under the seigneurial system of land ownership used in France. By 1792, Britain had taken over this area and began opening land to settlements. However, huge tracts of land were owned by absentee proprietors creating a situation where enterprising individuals and families could set up farming on land without any overhead expenses - no purchase or lease arrangements, no taxes on assets or income, and no town structure to support churches and schools. Many Vermonters-particularly poorer families like the Youngman, Jones, and Whitcomb families-found it tempting to move slightly north over the American border to become squatters in the Eastern Townships. This Frontier period gave way to government and increased influence from the Church of England in the 1830s reducing the benefits to squatters and sending some back across the border.[3]

And, once again, Thomas and his family (most likely Tirzah, Lucinda, and Salley,) were warned out of a Vermont town. In 1816, the town of Washington selectmen ordered the constable to "summon Thomas Youngman and his whole family" to depart.[4] Apparently, Thomas was able to show that he would not be a burden to the town and was allowed to remain. He was a recorded landowner there from 1819-1826. (See Washington in Orange County map 5-1 in Chapter 5.) During this time, Lucinda married and moved to Quebec where five of her six children were born. The same year that Salley married, her father Thomas sold his land in Washington. It is possible that Tirzah died in this year as well.

The next record shows Thomas living with his daughter Betsey Whitcomb and her husband in Morristown in 1840 when the census recorded the names of Revolutionary War veterans receiving pensions. Thomas died 1 October 1842. Tirzah presumably died before 1840, and no burial site has been located for either Thomas or Tirzah Youngman. The Youngman family repeatedly moved to undeveloped, rural locations.

Thomas' adventurous spirit encouraged him to go to new areas, hopefully to improve his family's lot in life. In northern Vermont it is possible that Thomas undertook

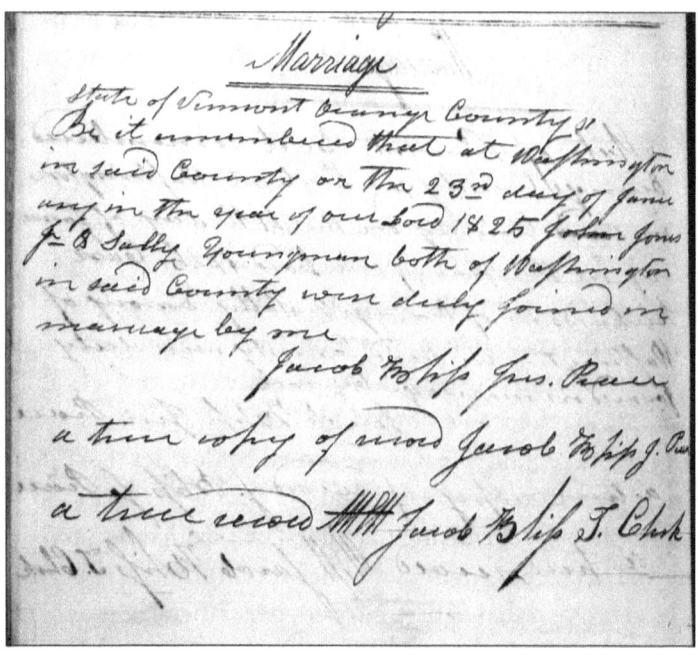

Marriage record of John Jones Jr. and "Sally" Youngman, 1825.[5]

lumbering tasks for salary in addition to clearing land for farming. Since the Eastern townships are characterized by rolling hills rather than the steeper terrain of northern Vermont, the land may have been more suitable for agricultural pursuits.

Meeting the Joneses

Interestingly, sisters Salley and Lucinda both married men named John Jones, of similar ages, and, possibly, both came from Washington, Vt. - maybe even cousins. The little we know about Lucinda's husband comes from the 1850 and 1860 censuses that report he was born in approximately 1790 and in the state of Vermont. By 1823, John and Lucinda had moved to Canada.

As it turns out, there were numerous John Jones who migrated to or were born in Washington (Orange County), Vt. after the town was incorporated in 1792. Washington had one main road through it and several creeks, but no major river to aid transportation or the development of industry. During the early settlement of the town, the records show that each John Jones, who moved to town or became of age to own land and participate in town affairs, was assigned a suffix number that did not designate familial relationship. The 1810 census enumerated three John Jones - John Jones, John Jones 2nd, John Jones 3rd - and these designations were also used in vital records. A look at the ages of these men shows that John Jones and John Jones 3rd were father and son whereas John Jones 2nd was probably a nephew - likely a son of Ephraim, an older brother of John (1st). This numbering system carried over into the land records where the father/son relationship was confirmed. However, when

Looking south down VT-110 in Washington, Vt. Photo by author.

Westward view from VT-110 of Calef Library and the Unitarian Universalist Congregation Church, Washington, Vt. Photo by author.

View from VT-110 near the Town Hall, Washington, Vt. Photo by author.

John 3rd returned to Washington he was labelled John "Jr." in the land records suggesting that John Jones 2nd had left town.

John Jones Jr., whose family Salley married into, and his siblings, were born in Goffstown, N.H. His father, John Jones (either Sr. or 1st), moved to Goffstown shortly after his marriage to Abigail Barnard. John and Abigail Jones had moved 40 miles west from the Hawke/Kingston, N.H. area where his father Nathan Jones lived. In 1797, John leased land in Washington, Vt., and he moved his family there. By 1800 many New Hampshire Joneses had relocated – John's oldest son Stephen and wife; older brother Ephraim and family; sister Miriam who married in Washington. John Jr. married a local woman, Margeret Nelson, and their first child Barnard was born in 1806. In 1811 he sold his land and moved his wife and two sons to Candor, Tioga County, N.Y. where he is listed on the 1820 census with his wife, three boys and four girls under 15. By 1823 he was back in Washington, where he purchased land for himself. Additionally, John Jr. agreed to assume the lease for the land his father had been leasing from the town since 1797. In exchange, the senior John and Abigail Jones received the right to live there for their natural lives.

Salley Youngman Jones

Salley Youngman likely arrived in Washington with her parents and was part of the "family" that was warned out in December of 1816. Salley was not enumerated with Thomas in the 1820 census and Thomas' pension deposition the same year states that he and Tirzah were in dire straits and on their own. Salley did marry John Jones Jr. in

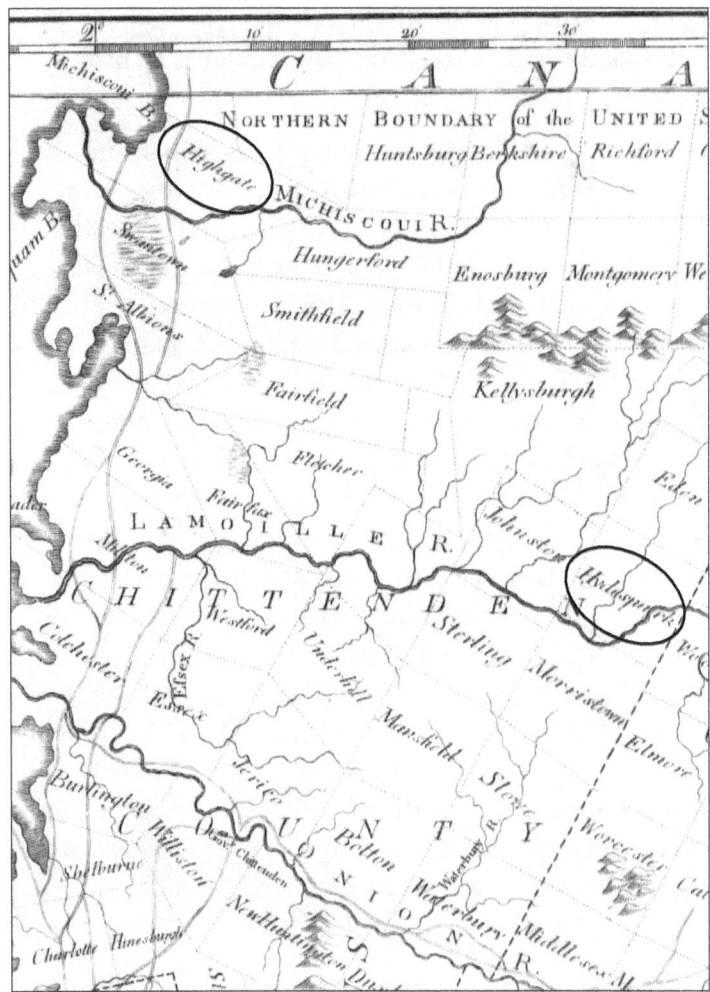

Map 6-2. Lamoille County with Highgate and "Hydespark" circled. Vermont (cropped), 1796. Courtesy of David Rumsey Map Collection.

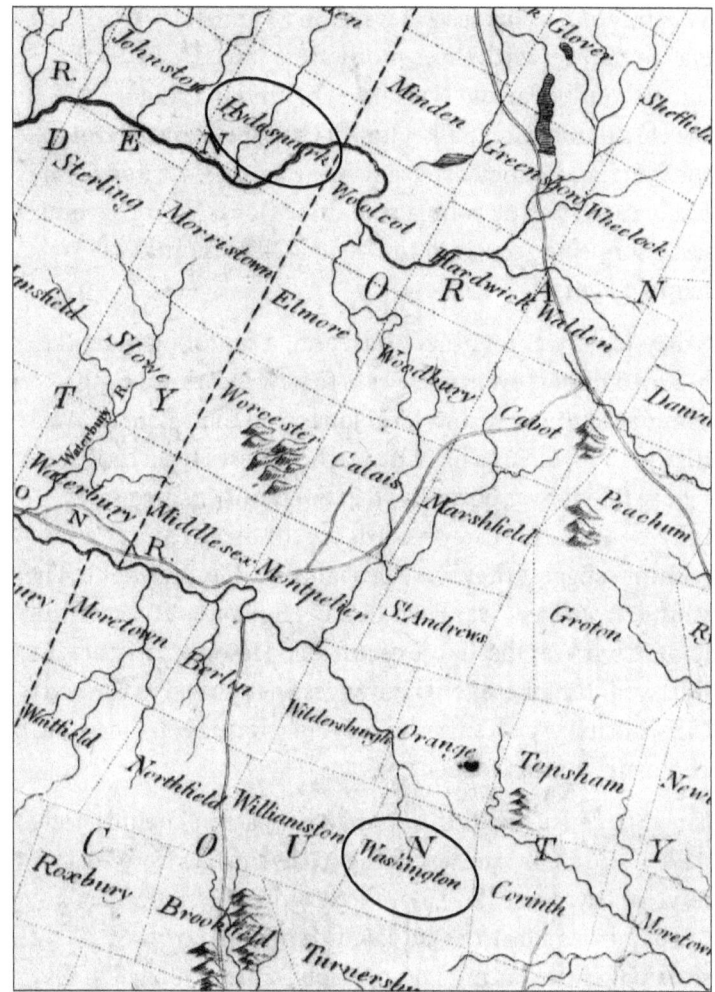

Map 6-3. Orange County with "Hydespark" and Washington circled. Vermont (cropped), 1796. Courtesy of David Rumsey Map Collection.

Washington, as his second wife, on 23 January 1825. Jones was a widower with three motherless sons. He had left a fourth son, 3 year-old Nathaniel, behind in Candor, N.Y. in the care of his sister Sally (Jones) Campbell. At the time of the marriage, Salley's stepsons were aged 18, 12, and 6. She likely cared for the youngest of these, John N., for several years while he grew into adulthood. Nine months later Ezra was born.

Salley Jones went with her husband, a rambling man like her own father, every few years to new locations. Both Thomas Youngman and John Jones sold their land in Washington in 1826. For a brief time, the Joneses lived in Canada where Edwin was born. By 1830 the family was counted in Hyde Park, Vt. Later records for the girls, Pauline and Almina, suggest they were probably born in Vermont. The youngest, Alfred, was born 1841 in Highgate, Vt. according to his Civil War discharge certificate. However, neither of the two John Joneses or their wives were found in the 1840 U.S. census, which suggests they may have been living near Highgate, but in Canada.

The 1850 census finds the Youngman sisters, Lucinda and Salley, and their families living in the upstate New York town of Lawrence (St. Lawrence County) where Salley's husband was a farm hand. Lucinda's husband was a shoemaker– a common occupation in the extended Jones family.

Yet, ten years later, John and Salley returned to Hyde Park where John continued as a farmer. There was an overlap in the census-taking as Almina is recorded with her husband Hiram Sereno Haskins and two daughters, as well as being listed as part of her parents' household. Edwin and his family lived nearby, as did John N., his wife and daughter, and their married daughter Sophia. Ezra, his wife, and four children also lived in Hyde Park. John Jones died in 1862 (burial unknown) and Salley died 1 May 1866 and was buried in Hyde Park, the home-town of her five Jones offspring, one step-son, and their numerous descendants.[6]

Looking at the remote northern region where Salley spent much of her childhood, one can imagine that the women in Thomas Youngman's household had to be industrious and self-sufficient. Certainly, their daily routines were focused on staying warm in winter, hauling water, growing produce, raising livestock, and "making do" with clothing and supplies on hand. Salley, her sisters, and her mother were true pioneering women of an American frontier.

Four generations later, Salley's great grand-daughter, Laura Mary Brown, having left the Vermont county of her ancestors, married George Everett Ingalls, whose great grandmother was Sally Safford of Brighton, Massachusetts.

Holbrook Cemetery, Hyde Park, Vt. with Salley Jones' headstone inscribed "Salley wife of John Jones." Photos by author.

End Notes

1. Thomas Youngman, Revolutionary War pension, New Hampshire, S41396, M804, RG 15, *Case Files of Pension and Bounty-Land Warrant Applications based on Revolutionary War Service compiled ca 1800-ca 1912, documenting the period ca 1775-ca 1900*. Fold3.com.

2. Barnet Town Records, Deeds vol. 1, 1783-1791, p221, 6 June 1787, "Lucretia Youngman," FHL#008129461, image 393.

3. J. I. Little, *"In the desert places of the wilderness": The Frontier Thesis and the Anglican Church in the Eastern Townships, 1799-1831*, Department of History, Simon Fraser University, Burnaby, B.C., 2002.

4. Washington Town Records 1769-1866, v2, p. 117, "Summons Thomas Youngman," FHL#5427875, image 231. Note: The state of Vermont no longer allowed the practice of "warning out" in 1817; Wikipedia.org.

5. Washington Town Records 1769-1866, v2, p. 216, "Marriage," FSL#5427875 image 304.

6. Priscilla L. Partridge, "The Elusive Daughters of Thomas Youngman, A Revolutionary War Patriot," *Vermont Genealogy* (Vol. 24, No. 2, Spring 2019) and "The Lost Siblings of Ezra C. Jones of Hyde Park, Vermont," *Vermont Genealogy* (Vol. 21, No. 1, Spring 2016).

Chapter 7
The Sally Vignettes... Safford and Everett

Sally Safford 1768-1838

Sally Safford was the middle child and the only known daughter of Thomas and Sarah (Kettell) Safford. She was likely called Sally to differentiate her from her mother, Sarah, as her grandmother Sarah Blanchard Kettell had died before young Sally's birth.

Sally's baptism was recorded on 14 July 1771 in the Roxbury (Massachusetts) Church records. However, Sally's death record states she was born in 1768, so she was clearly a young girl living in the hotbed of American patriotism. Her father, Thomas Safford, was named on the Muster Roll of Capt. Samuel Barnard's Company in Thomas Gardner's Regiment of Militia that marched from Watertown to Lexington when the alarm was sounded on 19 April 1775. Colonel Gardner went on to fight at the Battle of Bunker Hill in June where he was mortally wounded. He was then brought to the house of his sister, Mrs. Elizabeth (Gardner) Sparhawk, in Brighton where he died.[1] Similar to the marital family of Salley Youngman, four older brothers of Sally Safford's future husband answered the Lexington Alarm and continued their involvement in the ensuing Revolutionary War. Their father, Israel Everett Sr, also responded to the Lexington Alarm.[2]

Thomas Safford was born in Boston, Mass. to Nathan Safford and Lydia Stetson. Thomas's mother died shortly after his birth and his father died when Thomas was thirteen. He was assigned a guardian but the lack of parents likely contributed to a sense of instability that other young men might not have experienced. At age 18, Thomas was a resident of Watertown, which was located eight to ten miles westward of Boston. He joined Capt. Jonathan Brown's Company during the Lake George Campaign of the French and Indian Wars (aka Seven Years War).

Thomas Safford then moved forty miles south to Dedham, where in April of 1764 the Dedham selectmen ordered him to leave town within 14 days. Apparently they were concerned with Thomas Safford's residential and economic situation and feared having him become the responsibility of the town. However, when Thomas married Sarah Kettell of Medford, Mass., in Medford on 31 July 1764, he was described as from Dedham. And then in October of the same year, the Dedham selectmen issued warning out orders for Sarah Safford and a man named Moses Souter who lived with Thomas Safford. Once again, the transient concern was resolved as the Saffords were listed as residents of Dedham in 1766 when Mrs. Sarah was admitted into the First Parish Church and where son Thomas was christened.[3] The family then moved forty miles northeast, where Sally and a second brother, Benjamin, were baptized in the Roxbury Church.

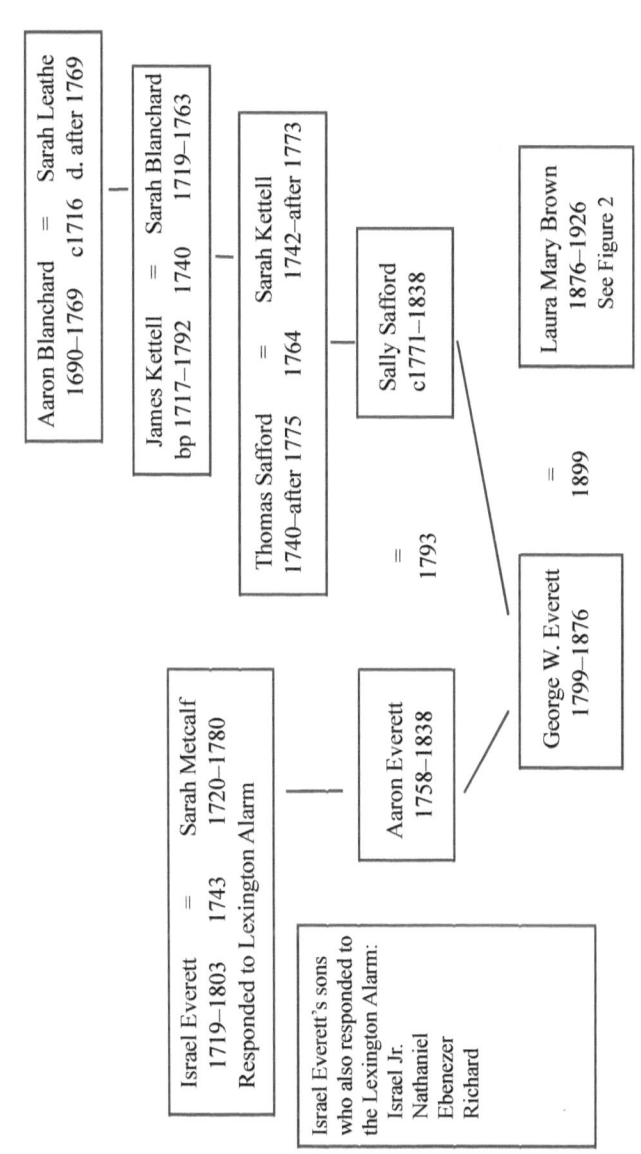

Figure 7. Line of Descent to George W. Everett through three Sallys (maternal line).

The Safford family next settled in Watertown. In the early days of the Revolutionary War, Thomas served as a private in Col. William R. Lee's Independent Company of Continental Troops, which was organized in Cambridge, Mass. on January 12, 1777.[4] After that, Thomas Safford can be found in the Watertown town records – he requested reimbursement from the town for the care of a transient woman; he requested payment for repair of the minister's fence; and he owed the town for the Ministerial Tax. As Thomas Jr. would not have been of age until 1787, these records can be attributed to the father. Unfortunately, we don't know how long Sarah Kettell Safford was in partnership with her husband, but, her daughter, Sally Safford, married into another hardworking and patriotic Massachusetts family.

The Everett Family

Aaron Everett was born the seventh son of Israel Everett Sr. and Sarah Metcalf on 18 November 1758 in the town of Dedham. Israel and two sons, Israel Jr. and Nathaniel, responded to the Lexington Alarm on 19 March 1775 as Minute Men from Dedham although the sons served in a different unit from their father. Sons Richard and Ebenezer had already relocated to Watertown, where they also joined Col. Thomas Gardner's regiment destined for Lexington. Aaron would have been seventeen at this time – old enough to run the farm in his father's absence – yet too young for military service.

At some point, young Aaron left his father and Dedham, and moved north to Watertown where his brothers lived. Aaron may have met Sally Safford in Watertown through his brothers' regimental contacts or even earlier during

The Sally Vignettes...Safford and Everett

Thomas Safford's first residence in Dedham. Aaron Everett and Miss Sally Safford, both of Cambridge, were married on 2 April 1793 by Stephen Dana, Esq. Aaron was thirty-five and Sally was twenty-two years old.

Aaron Everett purchased roughly 90 acres, including land on the Charles River and some of the original land holdings of immigrant Nathaniel Sparhawk. The Everett parcels lay on both sides of the Great Road which connected Watertown to Boston at Massachusetts Avenue. The Great Road, now Western Avenue, crosses the Charles River in two places. This peninsula, or knob of land, that juts into the Charles River was initially part of Cambridge and called "South" or "Little Cambridge." After Cambridge refused to repair the bridge, the residents of the knob became part of Watertown and Newton until the area was incorporated as Brighton in 1807. Aaron's house was in the vicinity of Western Avenue and the current Everett Street, which was named after the family and was eventually extended further south towards Roxbury. In 1874, Brighton was annexed to Boston and is currently referred to as the Lower Allston neighborhood, whereas the current neighborhood of Brighton lies to the west.

Aaron grew to be a successful and diverse business man. Watertown town records show that Aaron leased fishing rights on his river frontage, paid taxes on pasture land, and lent money to the Watertown government. Middlesex County Probate records for the 1790s, show that Aaron appeared on the inventory lists of debts owed by several deceased Watertown men. One of these deceased debtors was a tanner, which aligns with Aaron's businesses involving cattle and other livestock.

In the purchase deeds and mortgage deeds for the Brighton

PIONEERS, FARMERS, AND PATRIOTS

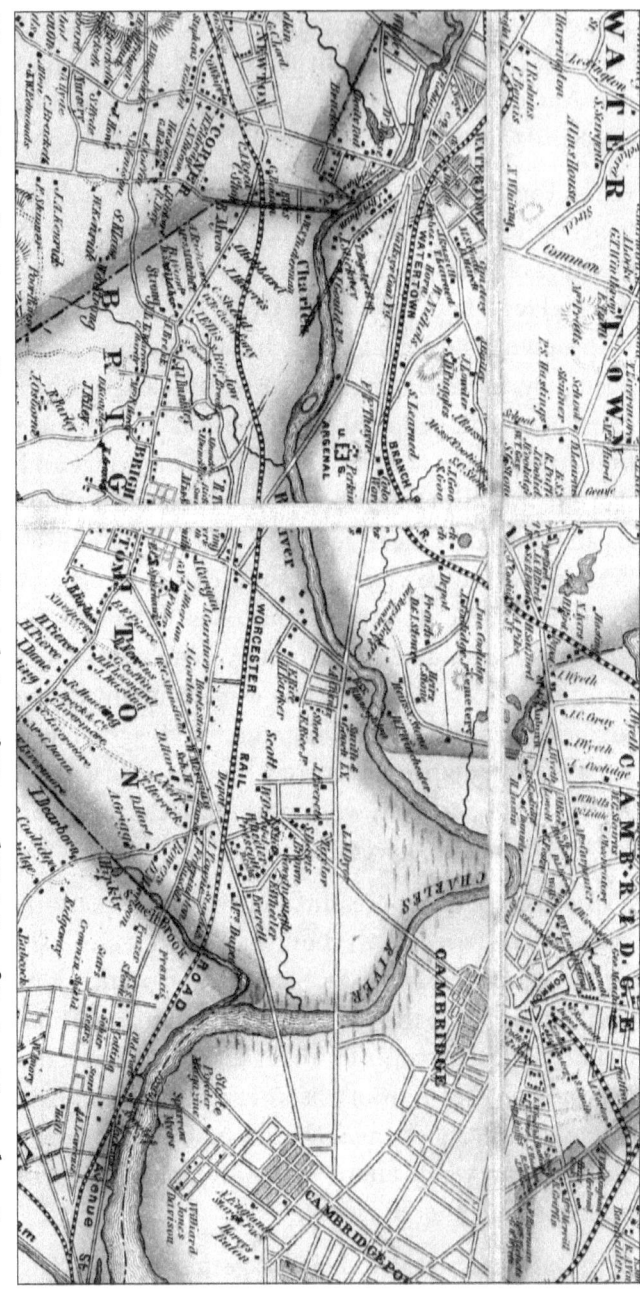

Map 7. Brighton showing two Everett properties. Partial view of City and Vicinity of Boston Massachusetts, 1852. Courtesy of David Rumsey Map Collection.

parcels, Aaron was described as a "victualler," an eighteenth century term for someone who procures or obtains supplies and provisions (like food). Prior to the Revolution, the British Navy brought all provisions needed for the sailors and officers from England on separate ships called "victualler ships." The Brighton-Allston Historical Society shares that a Cattle Market was founded in 1776 in Little Cambridge by a local landowner to feed George Washington's Continental Army.[5] Little Cambridge is where Aaron Everett acquired land, resided, and carried out his business interests. He likely participated in livestock raising, slaughtering, and butchering.

Later, military records show that Aaron Everett performed service at Boston and vicinity, "detailed for special duty," under Lt. Col. A. Binney's regiment in November of 1814. Possibly, he supplied meats to the regiment during the War of 1812. Construction of a railroad through Brighton, and across the Everett property, in the nineteenth century encouraged a huge growth in the cattle market there and the associated slaughtering and butchering required to prepare meats for sale; however, the Everett family had either passed away or moved elsewhere before this industry became dominant in Brighton.

By 1817, Aaron had achieved the title of yeoman. When Aaron began selling off his land, his wife released her dowers rights using either name, Sarah or Sally. Apparently they were not particular about what she was called, but Aaron insisted that "victualler" be struck out and replaced with yeoman before he put his name to one deed. Aaron eventually sold his land to his son Abner, who alongside brother Joseph, began to sell off pieces along Western Avenue and Everett Street for housing. It seems that son

Page 28 from Joseph Everett's probate showing land sold at auction by Abner Everett. Several lots were purchased by Aaron Jr. See note 6.

George W. Everett had no interest in the family businesses as he went into the trade of paper hanger, first in Boston proper and later in Chester, N.H. However, in 1835, George was drawn into the family real estate business as part of a promissory note with his brothers, Abner and Joseph, on a mortgage which was paid off by 1840.

Aaron and Sally Everett died within two months of each other in 1838. Of their seven children: Maria married a local widower whose wife had been a personal friend, and remained in the Brighton-Boston area. Maria Everett Herrick named a daughter, Sally Safford Herrick, after her mother and possibly in memory of her sister, Sally. Only a birth record for Aaron and Sally's daughter Sally has been found suggesting that she died as a child.

Joseph Everett, a widower, died in Brighton in 1856 without a will. His brother, Abner, was chosen administrator for Joseph's considerable estate which included lots on the Charles River as well as lots on the original family property at Everett and Western Drive. The proceeds went to remaining siblings–George, Aaron, Maria and Eliza.[6]

Aaron Everett, Jr., died in 1862, and he also appointed Abner to be the executor of his estate. By this time, Abner had followed one of his sons to California. With the consent of the widow, the siblings and the Court, George Everett became the executor. George's signature can be seen throughout the probate. The detailed inventory included in the probate shows that Aaron was heavily involved in horticultural pursuits and owned assorted harnesses, plows, and wagons necessary to farming operations.[7]

Eliza, the youngest, remained in Brighton through the deaths of her brothers. She died unmarried in Laconia N.H.

Geo. Everett signatures from estate documents for his brother, Aaron. See note 7.

Request by heirs of Aaron Everett to change executor to George Everett. See note 7, p5.

	Amount brought Forward	475.25
8	Tons English Hay	144.00
181	Chain wagon	5.00
	Drag	2.50
2	Harness & Whiffletrees	6.00
	Hand wagon	5.00
1	Sled	10.00
	Rubbish in Cellar	5.00
1	Pump	1.00
	Lot Manure	40.00
	Horse Cart	4.00
	Manure wagon & Ladders	75.00
	Market wagon	40.00
	Little wagon	5.00
	Pung	10.00
	Saddles Bean Idles & Jack	4.00
	Carriage & Robe	15.00
	Grey Horse	25.00
	Bay Horse	100.00
	Cow	80.00
	Feed & Grain Box	1.00
House Cellar	Apples	40.00
	Boxes	2.00
	Carrots	8.00
	Beets	8.00
	Potatoes	10.00
	Churn & Funnel	1.00
	Rubish	1.00
	Chest of Seeds	2.00
		1119.75

Partial inventory of Aaron Everett's belongings, listing horses, associated horse equipment, and produce stored in the cellar. See note 7, p19.

		Engine Wagon	50.00
	No 2	Lumber	6.00
Seed Barn		Pres	2.00
		Old Mats	.50
		Bath Tubs	.50
		Sail Cloth	3.00
		Rack & Bls	2.00
		Hand Barrow	2.00
		Corn & Rubbish &c	2.00
Barn		Grind Stone	3.00
		Sythes &c	1.50
	6	Manure Forks	4.00
	14	Shovels	4.00
	14	Hoes	4.00
	2	Iron	1.50
		Draft & Cow Chain	2.00
		Picks Spoons & Hammers	2.00
		Whiffletrees	1.50
	3	Ploes	6.00
	1	Cultivator	1.00
	1	Seed Sower	8.00
	5	Hay Forks	1.25
	4	Iron Rakes	1.00
	6	Strawberry Hoes	.75
		Seed Beans in 3 Bbls	8.00
		Rubish	1.00
		Wheelbarrow	2.00
		Axes	1.00
	2	Wood Saws	.50
	1	Sleigh	2.00
	1	Ox Yoke	1.00
		Cart Harness	10.00
		Lead Harness	5.00
		Plough &c	4.00

Partial inventory of Aaron Everett's belongings in the barn and seed barn, listing gardening tools, sleigh, ox yoke. See note 7, p21.

in 1884 where she had been living in a hotel operated by her nephew, George Henry Everett, a son of her brother George.

George W. Everett and his first wife Sarah Ellms, named two daughters Sarah, continuing a family tradition as well as honoring his wife. Sadly, both daughters died young. Later, George and his second wife had a daughter, Lucretia, who continued the "George" tradition by naming her son George Everett Ingalls - the future husband of Laura Mary Brown and the father of Miriam Lucretia Ingalls.

End Notes

1. See Thomas Safford in *Watertown's Military History*, authorized by a Vote of the Inhabitants of the Town of Watertown, Massachusetts, Boston: Published in 1907, under the Direction of a Committee Representing the Sons of the American Revolution, and Isaac B. Patten Post 81, Grand Army of the Republic, pp 78 and 114. For more detailed information on the people and history of Brighton, see J.P.C. Winship, *Historical Brighton*, vol. 1, (Boston: George A. Warren, 1899).

2. See Richard Everitt and Eben(ezer) Everett in *Watertown's Military History* (see note 1), pp 27, 75, 79, 86, 106. Israel Everett (Sr.) is honored for his service as a sergeant in the Militia from Dedham, Mass. (DAR ancestor A037834).

3. Robert Brand Hanson, *The Vital Records of Dedham, Massachusetts*, (Bowie, MD: Heritage Books, 1989).

4. U.S. National Archives, *Compiled Service Records of Soldiers who served in the American Army During the Revolutionary War*, M881, image 13054634, "Thomas Safford (Stafford)," accessed at Fold3.com.

5. Brighton-Allston Historical Society, website www.Bahistory.org. See also *Historical Brighton*, note 1.

6. Joseph Everett, 1856. *Middlesex County, MA, Probate File Papers, 1648-1871*, p31421:28, Vol: 30000-31999; americanancestors.org.

7. Aaron Everett, 1862. *Middlesex County, MA, Probate File Papers, 1648-1871*, p31414:5, 19, 12, 21 and 30, Vol: 30000-31999; americanancestors.org.

Chapter 8
Mim's Story:
A Descendant of Pioneers, Farmers, and Patriots

This compilation of stories of New England ancestors of Miriam Ingalls has spanned the eighteenth and nineteenth centuries. With Miriam's birth, we arrive at the first decade of the twentieth century. As with Miriam's female predecessors, the physical path of her adult life followed her husband's educational and career choices. Unlike her female ancestors, however, specifics relating to Miriam's childhood exist in diaries, letters, yearbooks, photographs and the ephemera of family collections as well as publicly accessible databases. Her personality can be more fully portrayed due to these documents, and the fact that she was personally known to the author.

As a married woman, Miriam returned to the land of her maternal and paternal ancestors. After a few years in Connecticut, Miriam's nuclear family moved to Massachusetts where they lived adjacent to her mother Laura's college girlfriend who had married her uncle's good friend. Miriam's son attended high school where his great-uncle had worked the farm and near the neighborhood schoolhouse in which his grandmother first taught.

Young Miriam

Directories and censuses show that Miriam's family remained in East Cleveland, Ohio for her youth but changed homes and neighborhoods every few years which must have been difficult for the children. Miriam's early childhood can only be gleaned from images in mother Laura's photo album–individual and group family poses, the family swimming in Lake Erie, numerous homes, camp scenes at the Young Men's Christian Association (YMCA) camps in Aurora and Silver Bay on Lake George, N.Y.

However, family ephemera provides an insight into Miriam's teen years. The Certificate of Scholarship (Girls) from East Technical High School issued June 15, 1923 lists coursework and grades for Miriam Ingalls. East Technical H.S. (ETHS) was the first public trade school in the Greater Cleveland area; one of five in the country when it opened in 1908. ETHS was co-educational until 1929 when it became an all-male school. During Miriam's attendance years, the school was a leader in interscholastic athletics, particularly city football championships.[1]

The report card was mailed to Miriam's home at 1823 Haldane Road, Cleveland. She was an average student overall. Interestingly, the classes she excelled in strongly resonate with the Miriam we knew and loved and the connection she and husband George shared. Miriam earned a 95 in U.S. History and 90 and 85 in general science and physics. (Her future husband earned his living as a science teacher and naturalist.) Miriam scored between 85 and 90 each of the three years she took Costume Design which included "construction and lettering, industrial design, nature drawing, color theory, color study, applied design,

Miriam (on far right) celebrating the 4th of July circa 1915.

Laura Ingalls with children: Miriam, Christine, Robert circa 1915.

Miriam in costume, possibly a class project, ca 1922.

Miriam and classmates modeling costumes, ca 1922.

and millinery design." These classes provide context for the outfits Miriam and her classmates were wearing in these photographs.

Miriam also achieved good grades in home-making and gymnasium; classes which set her up for life as a wife and mother, to George and their son, and for decades of outdoor summers as camp mother to countless boys. During those summers, she and the Ladies on the Point shared crafting ideas and patterns and excelled at knitting and sewing— baby clothes, sweaters and decorated sweatshirts for the grandchildren, clothes for Barbie dolls, plus both knitted and crocheted afghans.

Two autograph books from her high school years contain notes from friends and family. Christine, Robert, and Harold as well as mother Laura penned messages to Miriam. Christine, about age 12, wrote: "Dear Miriam: I thought and thought and thought in vain, And so I thought I'd write my name. Christine Ingalls." When Christine signed again in 1924, her penmanship had improved as well as her poetry.

Sept. 21, 1924
~~East Tech '27~~
Shaw 1926!

Dearest Sister,
"Smile!
And when you smile,
Another smiles,
And then there's miles
And miles of smiles,
And lifes' worth while
Because you smile!"
Loads of Love
"Sis"

Apparently, Christine was initially headed to Miriam's high school but changed plans to attend Shaw and graduate earlier.

Younger brother Bob, age 15, shared this:

> Mar. 31, 1921
> Dear Sister-
> People and pins
> Are useless when they lose their heads,
> Robert H. Ingalls

And finally big brother Harold, age 19:

> Dear Big Sister: 3/29/21
> You see I am very bashful so
> I will write in the back of the book.
> Poetry I cannot write-verse, I
> know not-but I can wish you the best
> wishes possible for the future, and in later
> years may all your troubles be little ones.
> Lots of Love from your "cub"
> reporter brother,
> Harold

Inside the 1923 edition of the ETHS yearbook, the *June Bug*, we find that Miriam was involved in many groups. She was Vice President for the fall semester of The Friendship Club, a girl's organization affiliated with the YWCA (Young Women's Christian Association). It held social, business, and inspirational meetings, initiation parties for new members, and events with the YMCA boys (Young Men's Christian Association). During the spring semester, Miriam was Secretary of the Palladium—a group that shared learning about far-away places and performed important service projects for the school. The Trojans was a small co-ed group that enjoyed fellowship and hiking and an annual house party at a summer cottage on a lake near Akron. Miriam was Vice President for the fall semester. Also mentioned on her class picture page were Girls Gym Captain, President of Home Room, Student Council, and Senior Social Committee.[2]

A surprising and heartwarming discovery was Miriam's role in the East Technical High School Reserve Officer's Training Corps (ROTC) led by Major Burton W. Phillips, the faculty member in charge of military training. Most baffling to her descendants had been the ROTC pin found in her belongings. But perusal of mother Laura's photo album shed light on the pin. Numerous photos showed Miriam in uniform wearing a cap with the pin, alone and with with three other young ladies; several young men and an older man in uniform; and parade ground drills.

A look into the history of the ROTC only added to the confusion, since ROTC was begun in 1819 by Capt. Alden Partridge, a former superintendent at the U.S. Military Academy at West Point, N.Y. Capt. Partridge established an academy in Norwich. Vt., now called Norwich University, which focused on college level military training. Several other institutions had begun military training, and then the Land Grant Act of 1862, sponsored by Vermont's Justin Morrill, required colleges established on public land to offer military tactic classes. The Plattsburg Movement began at a camp in northern N.Y in 1916–1917 where civilians were being trained in military preparedness due to concerns that the U.S. would not be effective if drawn into

Miriam Ingalls' ROTC pin from her cap. Photo by author.

Captain Miriam Ingalls and Lt. Col. Inman Cook.

Captain Miriam Ingalls 3rd Battalion.

Major Burton W. Phillips (on left) and Captain Miriam Ingalls (second from right) in a group photo.

Captain Miriam Ingalls and fellow co-sponsor.

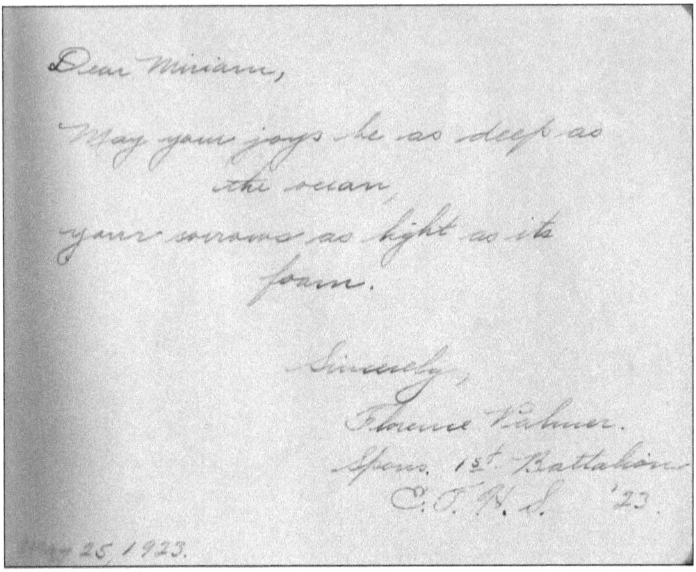

Dear Miriam,

May your joys be as deep as
    the ocean,
your sorrows as light as its
    foam.

    Sincerely,
    Florence Palmer.
    Spons. 1st Battalion
    C.T.H.S.   '23.

May 25, 1923.

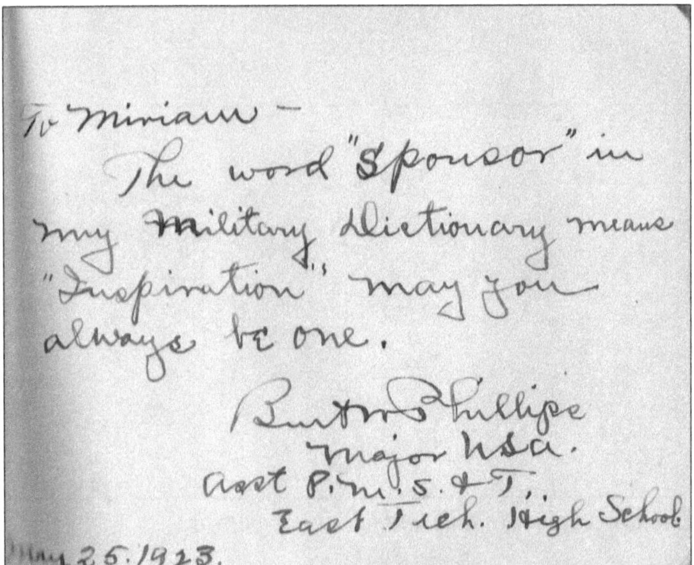

To Miriam –
    The word "Sponsor" in
my Military Dictionary means
"Inspiration", may you
always be one.

    Burton Phillips
    Major U.S.A.
    Asst P.M. S. & T.,
    East Tech. High School

May 25. 1923.

Dear Myrian,
   Take the word "glove"
And remove the "g"
   And keep what left
      "love"
As a sincere gift from
      Marguerite Wachob
         Sponsor
            P.I.H.

May 28, 1923

   When a sponsor is picked to represent a school they pick the best looking and the goodest girls. I don't believe Tech could have got better ones any place.
      Sergeant Brown
         now holding your
            horse.

World War I. Many colleges set up ROTC units as a result of the National Defense Act of 1916, for the purpose of training officers. Apparently, the Act of 1916 authorized high schools to operate Junior ROTC units at public and private educational institutions as well as college level.[3]

However, the East Technical High School program did not appear to use the terms "Junior" or "JROTC" in 1923.[4] Miriam and three female friends were key to the program, were given ranks, trained with the men, but were called "sponsors." Miriam's autograph books tell more of the story.

> *To Miriam-*
> *The word "sponsor" in*
> *my Military Dictionary means*
> *"Inspiration" May you always be one.*
> *Burton Phillips*
> *Major U.S.A*
> *Asst P.M.S. &T.*
> *East Tech. High School*
> *May 25, 1923.*

The four Sponsors of ETHS ROTC in 1923 were Major Marguerite Wachob, Captain Florence Palmer 1st Battalion, Captain Lola Prentice 2nd Battalion, and Captain Miriam Ingalls 3rd Battalion.

Fellow classmate Louise Delb wrote the following in Miriam's autograph book:

> *5/31/23*
> *Dearest Miriam:*
> *When Miriam first her sponsor suit wore*
> *On the streetcar one bright May morning*

The people all stared and some of them swore
They never before knew there were soldier girls.
Of course you wouldn't expect them to know
Miriam wasn't really meant to be a soldier
But because of her sunny smile and ways
One day the boys of training told her
They wanted her always to look them over
Thus, became Miriam a sponsor
of our would be soldiers.
(You can't blame them, can you?)
Remember me always. A poor attempt at poetry by
Louise Delb

Maj. Wachob, Capt. Palmer, and Sgt. Brown wrote in her autograph book. Col. Fred Banko and Lt. Col. Inman Cook appear in photos with Miriam, her co-sponsors, and in larger group settings.

Additionally, the student Officers of the East Technical unit, created a club to encourage togetherness among the ROTC officers and to determine ideas for the betterment of the unit. A photo of the Club members in uniform and a listing of officers with ranks was included in the June Bug 1923.[5]

Considering the number of photos in Laura's album, one can only assume Laura B. Ingalls was proud of her daughter and the family shared in her success. At an ROTC picnic, the four Ingalls children were captured eating lunch together; Christine was caught watching a car being started; and Miriam can be seen hopping or dancing a jig with fellow cadets.

Miriam hopping with fellow cadets.

Miriam enjoying a picnic with siblings, Christine, Robert and Harold.

Mim's Story

College Life

On April 7, 1924, the spring following her high school graduation, Miriam received her acceptance letter to join the Freshman Class in the College of Arts and Sciences at Oberlin College. Photos capture Miriam and two young ladies in front of Memorial Arch at Oberlin College during High School or shortly thereafter. Miriam's older brother Harold was a student at Oberlin, graduating in 1926. Miriam's college plans went awry as stated in this delightful letter sent to her at Glenview Hospital in Cleveland:

> August ?, 1924
>
> Dear Miriam:-
>
> Your brother with the big grin and little moustache sent me all kinds of news in a letter which arrived this morning. He started out as though writing for the society column in a newspaper and finished with somewhat of a questionnaire. It was a fine letter though and I enjoyed it.
>
> Pete and his typewriter are like an aeroplane dropping bombs. Sometimes they hit you and sometimes they miss but they always start you going some way. Two of the bombs this time were to the effect that you had just been operated on and that you are not going to be at Oberlin this fall – all of which is sure news to me and not at all good news. I hope you have real nice nurses and some good way of keeping amused while you're in the hospital. I can't picture you quite – except in white bed – for I've never been in a hospital except for very short visits with sick people when there wasn't even time to look around. Perhaps you have neighbors? – or maybe you have flowers and a window where you can look out? This letter has orders to carry you my best wishes for a quick and full recovery as well as a pleasant time while shut in. If you don't find

them inside the envelope you may be sure they slipped out when you were opening it and take it for granted that they are all in the air around you now. As to your not being at Oberlin this fall we shall all be disappointed and will hope harder than ever to have you with us the next year. Would you not like to be a freshman when Pete, Jack, Bob, and I are all wise seniors ruling the campus and trying to keep our big heads under ordinary sized hats? Seriously, I am very sorry that your mother is in poor health and sincerely hope she will get better. We all hope that you will be able to visit Oberlin several times during the year, at least, and we count on having you there a year from this fall.

Ted Abbott's missive continues to entertain with a description of his drive home to Connecticut with a professor in the professor's Ford and the subsequent activities which kept Ted busy at the family home in Woodbury. Paying jobs were scarce that year. Brother Harold provided constant support for Miriam's college career. For her birthday in 1923, Harold gave Miriam a book titled Oberlin Songs: "To my sister Miriam Ingalls with the hope that through singing these songs the Oberlin Spirit may be known to her. Love Harold B. Ingalls 12/17/23."

Certainly, Miriam's mother provided comfort to Miriam during her hospital stay and recuperation in 1924 and surely Miriam reciprocated during the last days of her mother's life. But sadly, Mrs. Laura B. Ingalls, succumbed to pulmonary tuberculosis and asthma on 19 May 1926 at the age of 49 leaving her husband George, three young adults-Harold, Miriam, and Robert-and one teen, Christine. Nineteen twenty-six was a tough year for the Ingalls family-grandmother Lucretia Underhill Everett Ingalls had died in January while staying with family in Berea, Ohio.

Miriam August 16 1922.

Miriam circa 1925.

Miriam and George Partridge.

Both women were sent to the Walnut Grove Cemetery in Methuen, Massachusetts for burial.

After much delay, Miriam began her college career in the fall of 1926, too late to attend with her brother and his friends. Her college textbooks show that she resided in Keep Annex. A clipping from the Oberlin Review dated April 19, 1929 states that "Miriam Ingalls, '29, has not returned since vacation, but is staying at her home in Cleveland because of illness." Alas, a college degree was not to be hers. Although her picture can be found in the 1930 Oberlin yearbook, Miriam did not graduate with the class of 1930.

By then, she had met and married George L. Partridge. Miriam wore a four-tiered white chiffon dress, a cap-shaped veil bordered with Chantilly lace and carried a bouquet of white roses, valley lilies, and sweet peas. The newlyweds took a short boat trip and then spent two weeks camping on a remote lake with her husband's family in Monson, Maine. Thus, began a sixty-four year adventure.

The Essence of Mim

As it turned out, the honeymoon camping trip was only the first of pioneer adventures of Miriam's married life. She eventually spent 41 summers living in a canvas tent at a boys' camp in Vermont. Here, her interest and enjoyment of the natural world grew. Her homes always had a shelf off the kitchen window where she would feed and observe wild birds, particularly her favorite, the Northern Cardinal. The living room windows were lined with African violets which happily bloomed for her. Lilac shrubs and beds of iris could be found surrounding her home. Not surprisingly, Miriam's color preferences spanned purple to pink including the shades of violet, lavender, and lilac.

Newlywed Miriam I. Partridge honeymooning in a tent on a lake in Monson, Me., August 1929. Truly a pioneering woman!

Miriam's nurturing nature certainly became evident as a young girl caring for her ill mother. As a young wife and mother running her own household, Miriam was called upon to care for her nephews at various times during their childhood, and she was frequently immersed into the hectic domestic life of her husband's family. Her mother-in-law wrote: "A lovely letter from Miriam. She is the star writer of the family. She is a lovely girl and an ideal mother." Miriam was the devoted mother of one biological child, but became mother/grandmother to countless campers and young staff at the boys' camp. After twenty summers, she had earned the title of Camp Mother and held that until she retired.

The classes in costume and design were not wasted by Miriam. She became an accomplished and prolific knitter of blankets, sweaters, and doll clothes. Miriam always had a list of Barbie and Ken clothes to knit or stitch for her grandchildren and the young neighbor girls whom she often supervised after school. One immense project was a blanket/quilt made of 25 different knitted squares. Miriam also organized family members in the production of a more traditional sewn patchwork quilt for her first grandchild to marry. In her role as Camp Mother, Mrs. Pat mended and repaired clothing worn and torn by anyone at the camp as well as adding achievement and recognition patches for campers and staff. And she submitted an annual report describing her summer tasks and the end of summer inventory.

Involvement in her high school ROTC and other organizations allowed Miriam to demonstrate leadership skills as well as find belonging and support. Health issues that required operations were frequent in her young adult life, and arthritis plagued her later decades, certainly making it difficult for her to be active outside her home. However, Miriam was a member of the Fortnightly Women's Club in her community, and both Miriam and her husband were affiliated with the Trinitarian Congregational Church of Northfield and the local garden club. A huge commitment for Miriam and George was their appointment as Class Teachers for the Class of 1953 at Northfield School for Girls. Starting with the girls' freshman year, the class teachers were responsible for class organization such as meetings and elections and social events including dances, sporting events and chaperoning dates. These young ladies remained friends and stayed in contact over the years. In later years, the couple volunteered together at the Greenfield Medical Center assisting visitors on Saturday evenings.

Memories of Mim

My grandmother, "Mim," was the best. My siblings and I were her only grandchildren as she had only one child. For whatever reason, 1960's progressivism maybe, we called all our grandparents by their first names or by their nicknames, like "Mim" and "Pat." Mim's high school autograph books show that her friends and classmates often called her "Mimmie." Within our family, Miriam began going by "Mim" when her three-year old niece Barbara was having difficulty saying "Miriam" and it was suggested that Barbara try "Mim." (In 2016, Barbara was surprised to learn that she was the cause of the nickname – she thought she had always used Miriam!) George of course got his nickname "Pat" from Partridge or "Paaaatridge" as New Englanders are apt to say. Together they were Mr. & Mrs. Pat.

View of the Ladies dock on Lake Dunmore.

View of a platform that held a Camp Ladies' tent.

Author with her grandmother in front of Miriam's camp tent.

During her 41 summers as a staff spouse, Mim resided in a canvas tent placed over a wooden platform situated in a row of five "ladies" tents. The Ladies of Anwi Point had their own swimming dock on the lake where we girls spent our visits splashing and swimming. From Mim's tent, we could hear the waves gently lapping at the shore or, during the occasional storm, smashing loudly on the rocks. Whenever sister play became tense or testy, Mim would admonish us with "Don't quarrel girls." Confrontation and controversy were not part of Miriam's personality.

In addition to her mending duties, she most certainly added a motherly and friendly presence to the all-male camp. When asked how it was being a camper with his grandparents on the scene, my brother responded: "Awesome!" Dearest grandmother Miriam died in 1993 in San Rafael, California leaving a large, loving family and her husband of 63 years.

In Closing

A pioneering spirit lived within Miriam. With her family, she went swimming, boating, and camping, and as an adult she lived alone in a canvas tent by the shores of a Vermont lake for 41 summers. Having been raised in a family supportive of and dependent on the Young Men's Christian Association, her choice of high school activities showed that she could handle the juxtaposition of activities with the Young Women's Christian Association and her role as Captain Miriam Ingalls in the Reserve Officer's Training Corps. The images of Miriam in her ROTC uniform training with the boys and Major Phillips clearly demonstrate her sense of American patriotism and the pride of her family. And, finally Miriam's lifelong interest and enjoyment of the natural world, and gardening for food and for pleasure, evoke visions of the farmers in her heritage.

Even though Miriam's place of birth was in northeastern Ohio, a region claimed by the Colony of Connecticut as the Western Reserve and now the easternmost state in the Midwest of the United States, Miriam Ingalls embodied the pioneering, farming, and patriotic traits of her New England ancestors. Although much of the existing documentation favors the men, we are able to learn, recognize and appreciate that these women have been traveling, toiling, and sharing in belief systems in support of their families throughout the previous centuries.

End Notes

1. "East Technical High School," Encyclopedia of Cleveland History, Case Western Reserve University, https://case.edu/ech/articles/e/east-technical-high-school, accessed 28 April 2024.

2. 1923 ETHS *June Bug*, Cleveland Public Library Digital Gallery, https://cplorg.contentdm.oclc.org/digital/collection/p15034coll1/id/17920/rec/1, accessed July 2025.

3. "Making the Best Military Officers in the World," History, https://armyrotc.army.mil/history/ and "Army Junior ROTC Program Overview," U.S. Army Junior ROTC, https://www.usarmyjrotc.com/army-junior-rotc-program-overview/ both accessed 26 June 2024.

4. See note 2, p. 14.

5. See note 2, p. 14.

INDEX

Abbott, Ted 145-146
Aldrich-Ames, Mattie Morse (Ingalls) 31
Amesbury, Mass. viii, 21, 73, 76, 78, 81 84
Anatolia College, Turkey (in Greece) 17
Argentine, Kansas 28

Baldwin, Algier 40
Banfill, Hannah, *See* Hannah Dearborn
Banfill, Hugh 84, *85*, 86
Banfill, John, immigrant *85*
Banfill, John (I) *85*, 86
Banfill, John (II) *85*, 86
Banfill, John (III) 84, *85*, 86
Banfill, Sally (Mrs. Nathan Davis) 40, *43*, 71, 84, *85*, 86, 90
Banfill, Sarah (maiden name unknown; Mrs. John Banfill II/Jr.) *85*, 86
Bangor, Maine 48, 46
Barnard, Abigail (Mrs. John Jones Sr.) *53*, 101, 105
Barnet, Vt. 94, 97-98
Bartlett, Lillian, *See* Lillian Jones
Bellevue, Ohio 28
Bellows Falls, Vt. 22, 24
Blanchard, Aaron *115*
Blanchard, Sarah, (Mrs. James Kettell) 113, *115*
Blood, Simeon 94, *96*
Boston, Mass. 45, 72, 94, 114, 117, *118*, 119, 121
Bradford, Vt. viii, 75, 78-79, 81, *83*, 86
Brighton, Mass. 109, 113, 117, *118*, 119, 121, 123
Brown, Alice (Beach) 31
Brown, Betsey, *See* Betsey Burgin
Brown, Clayton H. (C.H.) 3, 6, 8-9, 12-14, 16, 31, 40, 44, 129
Brown, Harvey M. 40, *43*, 44, 46, 90
Brown, Henry B. 48
Brown, Ira A. 3, 6, 8, 27, 39, 40, *43*, 51, *53*, 65, 71, 90
Brown, Ira Raymond 8, 9, 40
Brown, John *43*, 44-46
Brown, Laura (daughter of Clayton H. Brown) 3
Brown, Laura E. (Mrs. A. Moody) 3-4, 6, 9, 12-14
Brown, Laura Mary (Mrs. George E. Ingalls, "mother") 1-3, *4*, 6, 7, 8-9, 12-14, 15, 16, 21-22, 25, 26, 27, 28, 31, *32*, 34-36, 39-40, 44, 46, 48, 51, 54, 109, *115*, 126, 129, 130, *132*, 134, 136, 143, 146
Brown, Manly H. 46, 48
Brown, Mary (Mrs. Capt. Samuel Dearborn) *85*, 86, *89*
Brown, Mary Jones, *See* Mary M. Jones
Brown, Phylinda/Philinda, *See* Phylinda Davis
Brown, Samuel *43*, 44-45

Brown, Samuel B. 46
Brown, Sergeant *141*, 143
Brown, Thomas G. 46, 47, 48
Burgin, Betsy/Betsey (Mrs. John Brown) *43*, 44, 46

Cabot, Hyde 65
Cadys Falls, Vt. 40, 65, *66–67*
Cambridge, Mass. (including South or Little) 94, 116, 117, 119
Campbell, Sally (Jones), *See* Sally Jones
Candor, N.Y. 54, 105, 108
Chamberlain, Rebeckah 25
Chester, N.H. 21, 22, 44–46, 121
Choate, Humphrey 37
Cleveland, Ohio 25, 28, *30*, 130, 145, 150
Colby, Ezekiel (Jr.) 73, 74, 76, 80, 86
Colby, Capt. Ezekiel (Sr.) 73, 74
Colby, Miriam/Mary (Mrs. Joshua Davis) 73, 74, 76, 79, *80*, 84, 90
Colby, Sarah/Sally, *See* Sarah/Sally Fowler
Colby, Sarah/Sally (daughter of Ezekiel Colby Sr.) 73, 74
Compton, Carl and Ruth, Mr. and Mrs. 17–18
Concord (Rumford), N.H. *4*, 25, *29*, 72
Corinth, Vt. viii, 40, 44, 48, 72–73, *75*, 76, 78–79, 81, *82–83*, 84, 86, *87–89*, 90
Cutler, Mr. 12–14

Darling, A.P. (Alonzo Putnam) 6, 8, 9, 13–14, 21
Darling, Blanch 8, 31
Darling, Elsa (Mrs. Hiram C. Haskins) 52, *53*, 55
Darling, Ernest 8, 60
Darling, Mary Brown, *See* Mary M. Jones
Davis, David 79, 81
Davis, Dorothy, *See* Dorothy Hadley
Davis, Francis *80*
Davis, Joshua 43, *74*, 76, 78–79, *80*, 81, 90
Davis, Mary, *See* Mary Fowler
Davis, Miriam/Mary, *See* Miriam Colby
Davis, Nathan 40, *43*, 84, *85*, 86, 90
Davis, Phylinda/Philinda (Mrs. Harvey M. Brown) 40, *43*, 90
Davis, Ruth (Mrs. Ezekiel Colby Jr.) 76, *80*
Davis, Sally, *See* Sally Banfill
Davis, Samuel (Jr.) 79, *80*, 81, *82–83*, 84
Davis, Samuel (Sr.) *80*, 84
Davis, Simeon 76, 79
Dearborn, Godfrey *85*, 86
Dearborn, Hannah (Mrs. John Banfill III) *85*, 86
Dearborn, Capt. Samuel 78, *85*, 86, *89*
Dedham, Mass. 114, 116–117
Delb, Louise 142–143
Diggins Road, Hyde Park, Vt. 55, 62, 63, 68
Dow, Hannah (Mrs. William Fowler) *80*
Downing, Mehitable Braybrook 25
Dunstable, N.H. 93, *95*

Index

East Technical High School (ETHS), Cleveland, Ohio 130, 134, 136, 142, 143
Ellms, Sarah (Mrs. Aaron Everett) 126
Elmore, Vt. 8-9, 10-11, 52, 59
Emerson, Mary Jane (Mrs. Alvah Jones) 65
Essex County, Mass. 22, 24, 40, 72
Everett, Aaron 115, 116-117, 119, 121
Everett, Aaron (Jr.) 120, 121, 122-125
Everett, Abner 119, 120, 121, 123
Everett, Ebenezer 115, 116
Everett, Eliza 121, 123
Everett, George W. 22, 27, 115, 121, 122-123, 126
Everett, Israel (Jr.) 115, 116
Everett, Israel (Sr.) 37, 114, 115, 116
Everett, Joseph 119, 120, 121
Everett, Lucretia Underhill (Mrs. John A.G. Ingalls) 21, 22, 23, 24-25, 27, 31, 126, 146
Everett, Maria (Mrs. Herrick) 121, 123
Everett, Nathaniel 115, 116
Everett, Richard 115, 116
Everett, Sally (d. young) 121
Everett, Sally, *See* Sally Safford
Everett, Sarah, *See* Sarah Metcalf

Flanders, Lt. John 74
Flanders, Sarah (Mrs. Abner Fowler Sr.) 71-73, 74
Fowler, Abner (Jr.) 73, 74, 84
Fowler, Abner (Sr.) 72, 74
Fowler, Jacob 73, 74
Fowler, Mary (Mrs. Samuel Davis Sr.) 80, 84
Fowler, Sarah/Sally (Mrs. Capt. Ezekiel Colby) 71-73, 74, 76, 77
Fowler, William 80, 84
Franklin County, N.Y. 55
French, Joseph 94, 96

Gardner, Thomas 113, 116
Garfield, Vt. 5, 54, 60, 63, 64-65
Gill, Mass. 6, 9, 14
Goffstown, N.H. 54, 105
Green River Reservoir, Vt. 63-64

Hadley, Dorothy, (Mrs. Samuel Davis Jr.) 79, 80, 81, 84
Haskins, Adorno 52
Haskins, Chloe (Mrs. Ezra Jones) 8-9, 51-52, 53, 55, 56-57, 58, 60, 63-65, 68
Haskins, Elizabeth 52
Haskins, Hiram C. 52, 53
Haskins, Hiram Sereno 52, 63, 68, 108
Hatch, Roy 5, 6, 14, 16, 129
Haverhill, Mass. 76
Hawke (now Danville), N.H. 78, 81, 105
Herrick, Sally Safford 121

Highgate, Vt. 94, 98, *106*, 108
Hollis, N.H. 93-94, *95*, 97
Honey, Gideon *96*
Honey, Tirzah (Mrs. Thomas Youngman) *96*, 97-99, 105
Hooksett (Chester Woods), N.H. 44, 48
Hyde Park, Vt. viii, 3, 8-9, 39-40, 51-52, 54-55, *56*, 58, *59*, 60, 62, 63, 65, 68, 90, 93, *106-107*, 108-109, *110*

Ingalls, Carl 28
Ingalls, Christine R. (Mrs. Malcolm McKay) 28, *30*, 31, *33*, *35*, *131-132*, 134-135, 143, *144*, 146
Ingalls, George Everett 1, 3, 4, 8, 21-22, 25, *26-27*, 28, 31, 34, *35*, 36-37, 109, 126
Ingalls, Edmund 36
Ingalls, Harold "Pete" Brown 28, *30*, *33*, 34, 134-135, *144*, 145-146
Ingalls, Henry 21
Ingalls, John Addison Gurley 21-22, *23*, 25, *27*
Ingalls, Laura Brown (Mrs. George E. Ingalls), *See* Laura Mary Brown
Ingalls, Lelia (Snyder, "mom") 31, 34, 36
Ingalls, Lucretia, *See* Lucretia Everett
Ingalls, Marion Brown 22, 28
Ingalls, Miriam "Mim" Lucretia vii, 1, 16, *17*, 18, 28, *30*, 31, *32-33*, *35*, 71-72, 76, 126, 129, 130, *131-133*, 134-136, *137-139*, 142-143, *144*, 145-146, *147-149*, 150, *151*, 152-153, *155*, 156-157
Ingalls, Percy Howe 22
Ingalls, Robert Harding 28, *30*, *33*, *132*, 134-135, *144*, 146

Jones, Abigail, *See* Abigail Barnard
Jones, Abigail (Mrs. Hugh Banfill) 85
Jones, Alice 55
Jones, Alfred *53*, 55, 65, 108,
Jones, Almina (Mrs. Hiram S. Haskins) *53*, 60, 108
Jones, Alvah 65
Jones, Andrew 58, 65
Jones, Cora 58
Jones, Eddie M. 58
Jones, Edwin *53*, 58, 65, 108
Jones, Elsa/Elsie (Mrs. Taylor) 5, 55
Jones, Ephraim 101, 105
Jones, Ezra C. 3, 5, 9, 39, 51-52, *53*, 54-55, *56-57*, 58, 60, *61*, 63-65, 68, 108-109
Jones, George and Ann, 51, *See also* Ezra Jones and Chloe Haskins
Jones, John (2nd, not known if related to John Sr. and Jr.) 101, 108
Jones, John Jr. (3rd) *53*, 54-55, *56-57*, *96*, *100*, 101, 105, 108-109, *110*
Jones, John (Sr., 1st) 21, *53*, 101, 105,
Jones, John N. 108
Jones, Lillian (Mrs. Sydney Bartlett) 5, 58, 64
Jones, Lucinda, *See* Lucinda Youngman
Jones, Mary M. (Mrs. Ira A. Brown; Mrs. A.P. Darling) 3, 8-9, 13, *27*, 39-40, 43, 51, *53*, 54-55, 60, 65, 71
Jones, Miriam 105
Jones, Nathaniel 52, 54, 108

Index

Jones, Orvis 63, 65
Jones, Pauline (Mrs. Salmon Niles; Mrs. Hyde Cabot) 52, *53*, 60, *61*, 63, 65, 108
Jones, Salley, *See* Salley Youngman
Jones, Sally (Mrs. Campbell) 54, 108
Jones, Stephen 105
Jones, Wilbur 3, 65

Kettell, James 115
Kettell, Sally/Sarah (Mrs. Thomas Safford) 71, 113-114, *115*, 116
Kettell, Sarah, *See* Sarah Blanchard
Kingston (Kingstown), N.H. viii, 76, 78, 81, 84, 105

Lafayette, General Marquis de 46
Lake Dunmore, Vt. 134, 152, *154-155*, 156
Lamoille County, Vt. 51, 54-55, 58, *59*, 90, *106*
Lear, Mary Polly (Mrs. John Banfill I) *85*, 86
Leathe, Sarah (Mrs. Aaron Blanchard) 115
Longfellow, Lucretia, 23-24, See also Lucretia U. Everett
Lufkin, Stephen 37

Malone, N.Y. 52, 54-55
Martin, Susannah North 25
McKay, Ralph M. 31
McKay, Christine, *See* Christine Ingalls
McKinstry Hill (Mc'Kinstry Hill), Hyde Park, Vt. *57*, *62*, 63-65
Metcalf, Sarah (Mrs. Israel Everett Sr.) *115*, 116
Methuen, Mass. 6, 8-9, 12, 22, 150
Monson, Maine 150, *151*
Moody, Laura (Brown), *See* Laura E. Brown
Moors, Eddie 58
Morristown, Vt. vii, 8, 40, 52, 54-55, 58, *59*, 97, 99
Morrisville, Vt. *7*, 40, *42*, 58
Mount Hermon School, Gill, Mass. 6, 8-9, 12-14, 16-17

Nelson, Margaret (Mrs. John Jones Jr.) 54, 105
Newbury, Mass. 73
Newbury, Vt. 72-73, *75*, 78, *83*, 84
Niles, Salmon 63, 65
North School, Gill, Mass. 6
Northfield, Mass. 14, 16-18, 153
Northfield Seminary/Northfield School for Girls, Northfield, Mass. 6, 16, 153
Nottingham, N.H. 86

Oberlin College, Oberlin, Ohio 145-146, 150
Orange County, Vt. *61*, 72, *75*, 78, 99, 101, *106-107*

Palmer, Florence *140*, 142-143
Partridge, Ernest C. 17
Partridge, George Lewis 14, 16, 18, 31, *35*, 130, *149*, 150, 153
Partridge, Miriam Ingalls (Mrs. George L. Partridge, Mrs. Pat), *See* Miriam

165

Lucretia Ingalls
Partridge, Winona G. 16, 152
Pembroke, N.H. 44
Phillips, Major Burton W. 136, *139-140*, 142, 156
Pickering, Mary (Mrs. John Banfill, immigrant) 85
Pitts, Grace Josephine (Mrs. Roy Hatch) 6, 14, 16, *17*, 129
Portsmouth, N.H. 84, 86
Powers, Jonathan 37
Prentice, Lola 142
Prince, Sarah (Mrs. Lt. John Flanders) 71, 74

ROTC (Reserve Officer Training Corps) 136, *137*, 142-143, 152, 156
Rockingham County, N.H. 44, 86
Roxbury, Mass. 113-114, 117
Rumford, N.H., *See* Concord, N.H.

Safford, Benjamin 114
Safford, Lydia, *See* Lydia Stetson
Safford, Nathan 114
Safford, Thomas 37, 113-114, *115*, 116
Safford, Sally (Mrs. Aaron Everett) 37, 71-72, 109, 113-114, *115*, 116-117, 119, 121
Safford, Sarah, *See* Sally/Sarah Kettell
St. Lawrence County, N.Y. 54-55, 108
Salem, Mass. 3, *4*, 6, 21, 24, 36
Salem Normal School (Salem State University), Salem, Mass. 6, *7*
Salisbury, Mass. 72-73
Sanborn, David Jr. 37
Sanborn, Mr. J.C. *5*, 6, 12
San Rafael, Calif. 156
Sherer, David 94, *96*
Smith, Lizzie P. 60, *61*, 63
Snyder, Lelia (Mrs. George E. Ingalls, "mom") 31, 34, 36
South Hampton, N.H. 72
Sparhawk, Mrs. Elizabeth (Gardner; Mrs. Samuel Sparhawk III) 113
Sparhawk, Nathaniel 117
Stetson, Lydia (Mrs. Nathan Safford) 114

Taylor, Mrs. Elsie, *See* Elsa/Elsie Jones
Taylor, Mary (Mrs. Francis Davis) 80

Underhill, John 37
University at Burlington, Vt. 39

Wachob, Marguerite *141*, 142-143
Washington, Vt. 54, 75, 82, 99, 101, *102-104*, 105, *107*, 108
Watertown, Mass. 22, 113-114, 116-117
Wolcott, Vt. 40, *41*, 51, 54, 58, 60, 90
Wolcott, Oliver 40
Woodbury, Mrs. 8, 13-14
Whitcomb, Betsey (Elizabeth), *See* Betsey Youngman

Index

Whitcomb, Harriet (Mrs. Hiram C. Haskins) 52
Wright, Beulah (Mrs. Clayton Brown) 6
Wright, Charlotte (Mrs. Hiram C. Haskins) 52
Wright, Mary (Mrs Nicholas Youngman) *96*

YMCA (Young Men's Christian Association) 17, 25, 28, *29*, 130, 135, 156
Youngman, Abigail (maiden name unknown; Mrs. John Youngman) 94, 98
Youngman, Betsey (Elizabeth) (Mrs. Simeon Whitcomb) 98-99
Youngman, Ebenezer 94, *96*
Youngman, Jabez 94, *96*, 98
Youngman, John 94, *96*, 97-98
Youngman, Lucinda (Mrs. John Jones) 98-99, 101, 108
Youngman, Lucretia (probably Tirzah) 97
Youngman, Mary 94
Youngman, Nicholas 93-94, *96*
Youngman, Salley (Mrs. John Jones Jr.) *53*, 54-55, 71, 90, 93, *96*, 98-99, *100*, 101, 105, 108-109, *110*, 114
Youngman, Stephen W. 94
Youngman, Thomas 93, 94, *96*, 97-99, 105, 108-109
Youngman, Tirzah, *See* Tirzah Honey
YWCA (Young Women's Christian Association) 135, 156

www.ingramcontent.com/pod-product-compliance
Lightning Source LLC
Chambersburg PA
CBHW020415080526
44584CB00014B/1335